D0380379

CHASE JOYNT &
MIKE HOOLBOOM

YOU ONLY
LIVE TWICE

SEX, DEATH AND TRANSITION

COACH HOUSE BOOKS, TORONTO

Published with the generous assistance of the Canada Council for the Arts and the Ontario Arts Council. Coach House Books also gratefully acknowledges the support of the Government of Canada through the Canada Book Fund and the Government of Ontario through the Ontario Book Publishing Tax Credit.

LIBRARY AND ARCHIVES CANADA CATALOGUING IN PUBLICATION

Joynt, Chase, 1981-, author
     You only live twice : sex, death and transition / Chase Joynt and Mike Hoolboom.

ISBN 978-1-55245-331-5 (paperback).

     1. Marker, Chris, 1921-2012--Criticism and interpretation. 2. Joynt, Chase, 1981-. 3. Hoolboom, Michael. 4. Transgender people--Canada--Biography. 5. HIV-positive persons--Canada--Biography. I. Hoolboom, Michael, author II. Title.

PN1998.3.M366J69 2016   791.4302'33092   C2015-908200-5

You Only Live Twice is available as an ebook: ISBN 978 1 77056 449 7.

Purchase of the print version of this book entitles you to a free digital copy. To claim your ebook of this title, please email sales@chbooks.com with proof of purchase or visit chbooks.com/digital. (Coach House Books reserves the right to terminate the free download offer at any time.)

Names and places have been changed.
Only the stories remain.

'Culture is the translation … [of] the desire a person believes he can't afford to acknowledge.'

— Adam Phillips, *Eecoming Freud: The Making of a Psychoanalyst*

You Only Live Twice

Foreword

This is a collection of love stories between people and generations, sourced from the intersection of one man's transition from female to male and another's near death from AIDS in the 1990s.

I met Mike Hoolboom in 2011. Our relationship was initially routed through a shared passion for movie-making and a related interest in Chris Marker. It took me almost five years to realize that we were only talking about the French filmmaker to avoid vulnerability – first within ourselves and then within each other.

Prior to our first meeting, I found Mike on the cover of *NOW* magazine, the most circulated guide to arts and culture in Toronto. His film *Mark* was premiering at Hot Docs, the pre-eminent documentary festival in the city. *Mark* is a devastating portrait of Mike's friend and former editor Mark Karbusicky. In the film, Mike tries desperately – and aesthetically – to recover meaning and memories after Mark's suicide. The movie is about the impossibility and necessity of telling stories, and about the potentials of image, text and community as healing.

In an interview about *Mark*, Mike admitted that he was happiest in the editing room. The public was his platform, but perhaps not his priority. That same year, I learned of many intimate and personal connections Mark shared with the trans community in Toronto. Disparate worlds, again colliding.

This book is positioned in and around many relationships that have changed or are changing. The conversation contained within is a technology of profound intimacy, one that when rendered public will find new privacy again.

Of course we didn't invent this form; it's a refashioned novel with generous attention paid to the failures of non-fiction stories.

Arrows and signs point freely to incongruities, and to pieces and people long lost to love's unending process of revision.

This is a story about sex, death and transition; it is also a project about proximity that now requires incredible distances.

The unspoken promise was that in our second lives we would become the question to every answer, jumping across borders until they finally dissolve. Man and woman. Queer and straight. In this moment, we write about love. Shopping is a form of voting, and love is a way to topple the state, or at least to budge the inner states that have held us in thrall for too long.

For so many years we wanted only to come to the end.

To finish with it all.

To close the book.

First Life

'Let's face it. We're undone by each other. And if we're not,
we're missing something.'

– Judith Butler, *Undoing Gender*

Chris Marker died today. Heart failure, the death of kings. People are already gathering at the jetty in the Orly airport, an impromptu memorial for the French filmmaker as renowned for his secrecy as his movies. Half a dozen people, give or take, leaving origami felines to keep a discreet watch over the waiting areas. How did they all know to bring black roses? The news of Marker's death is not yet public, but somehow word has reached them, though each step they take has a hitch in it, a certain tentativeness, making space for the maestro's possible reappearance.

Why do they call airport buildings 'terminals'? Orly is a medium-sized hub; bright adverts offer blown-up versions of a better life, while languid scrums of travellers invent new ways to leave their bodies. Two men hover near the viewing portals. Even through their sadness they can hardly help but notice that they are wearing versions of the same coat. Slowly, as if reluctant to break the spell of grieving, one of them offers his hand and a few words of introduction. Chase Joynt. Mike Hoolboom. Mike looks like he's spent the last month sleeping in an abandoned motocross raceway while an eighteen-wheeler rolled over him. He's a tall stick of a man, with a shock of hair that would be white if he weren't so quick with the brown food colouring. There's something hollowed out in his features, as if he's presenting the remains of an archaeological dig. Chase is a couple of decades younger. He's covered in tattoos, and has the face of someone who might be considered easy-going, though the eyes are a giveaway, soft and brown and hurting. He's spent most of his life trying to let people in, all the while shutting them out.

Chase actually met Marker years ago in what could almost be described as a bar on New York's fearsome Avenue C –

even legends need to drink. Of course Chris Marker didn't say he was Chris Marker. That would be gauche, as they say on the left. Like Chase, Marker is a code breaker, irresistibly drawn to the relationship between culture and aesthetics as a key to resistance, a key that might unlock the prisons of standard time and state control that both men can feel coursing through their bodies. As a filmmaker with only a few titles stacked beside his name, Chase is only too aware that some of cinema's roads-not-taken have been cleared away by this maestro of the personal film essay, a form that Chase tries to take in his own directions. Meeting Marker was like saying hi to a cinema dad. Home and not home.

'But how did you know it was him?' Mike asks, looking for some trace of the encounter in his companion's face.

'Film studies loves a headshot,' Chase offers. 'I told him that I was also travelling with a new name and a new identity.'

'I'll bet that piqued his interest.'

'It was as if he already knew.'

In Orly, the two men retire to a recently evacuated lounge, opening toward each other despite themselves. They can already feel the contours of something familiar between them – it lives without a name, but it's a quality that lies at the root of what they like to call their personality. It has separated them from nearly everyone they've ever cared about. Only it's not separating them now.

Chase palms the smooth, pretend-vinyl surface of the moulded chair on which he is now sitting. When he looks up, there is something in Mike's drawn-tight skin that offers a question mark or two. He puts the black rose down on the seat beside him and pats it once, as it to keep it from straying. Mike aims himself toward a seat on the other side of the aisle, but that would put them shouting distance apart, so without giving it a second thought, as if he belonged there all along, he sets himself down beside this stranger and is greeted with the first of a series of smiles. Surprise doesn't begin to describe the feeling. More than a few years ago he decided to cap the guest list to the party of his life, but he really likes this guy. Besides, almost immediately they launch into one of his cherished fan fantasies, which is to describe Chris Marker's most perfect movie, *La Jetée* (*The Jetty*). Meaning: that in place of the awkward conversation between perfect strangers (what's so perfect about them?) they don't have any trouble opening the door of their shared obsession.

Chase starts in with a summary rap that can't help but feel rehearsed: 'Orly was the setting of Marker's monumental *La Jetée*, a 1962 flick composed almost entirely of black-and-white stills. It tells the story of a Paris in ruins; it wasn't only the ruling class that had lost the knack of getting along, the remainder were driven underground by radiation fallout, locked in a desperate countdown with dwindling resources. The last man who dreams in colour is chosen for time travel – neither young nor old, he has the kind of beauty that makes the viewer long to be ordinary. After securing rescue codes from the future, he is hunted down by state scientists and shot in the departure lounge. It was a moment he had seen as a boy, or at least caught glimpses of – it was his own death he had witnessed, and he had spent his life conspiring to return to that moment.'

Another mutual surprise shared: many of the important people in their lives are those they'd never met. The nameless man in Marker's film, for instance, the one who found his end here in the airport. It's as if they were both granted a wish to choose their own ghosts, their own customized hauntings. Chase marks off his companion's razor-sharp cheekbones, holding up eyes that are so tired. 'I could look like him one day,' he thinks resolutely. There is something missing in Mike's face, and Chase can almost touch it as he crouches over a heady cup of espresso. As Mike talks about the unnamed man in Marker's film, he might be talking about himself. Traditional readings of the film remark on the hidden shape of the subject's life as he rushes to meet an appointment with his own death, holding a mirror to his culture's self-immolation. But what keeps Marker's unnamed citizen orbiting the magnetic pull of Mike's own persona choices, what marks him as a citizen of a future Mike has already recognized as his own, is that the anonymous man died twice in the movie, once at the beginning and then again at the end.

'There's only one way a man could die after he's already been shot dead.'

'You mean?'

'He didn't live a double life. He lived twice.'

'Yes. Yes.'

As Mike purses his lips to produce a coffee orifice, Chase watches the last puzzle piece fall into place. He's seen this face before – well, not this face exactly, but faces just like it. It is the symptom of a life-saving drug cocktail that absolved a generation of HIV-positives from a certain death, though the cost was a form of fat redistribution. He struggles to find the medical term and comes up blank. Yes, as he looks across his new companion's world of skin, there's little doubt Mike is HIV-positive. Chase picks up the black rose and sniffs the odourless offering. How to say what can't be said? How to share the implicit understanding?

Chase locks eyes with his companion for a moment before finding an anonymous floor tile to absorb his attention. 'So many of my friends tested positive that I started feeling left out, like I would never be part of the union.' It is a lie, but also a truth. Mike dabs at an imaginary spot on his cheek, his face a new display room of fear and attraction. Chase puts each word down with a touch so light he might be seeding clouds. As if he were afraid to wake his listener.

Chase adds, 'I couldn't help noticing that for men and women of a certain generation, they had survived their own death.'

'Sometimes.' The word is sharp and short, spoken in a cemetery whisper.

'Sometimes,' Chase acknowledges, with a tone drop. 'I always connected them to this place, this airport in Orly.'

They wait until Mike produces the waited-for prompt. 'Why?'

'Because this is the primal scene of the second life, isn't it? I mean, for anyone who has lived and died and lived again, how can you help but think of the man in Marker's film who came here to die twice? It was a science-fiction film, a story of the future that turned out to be our future. It didn't mean that Marker lived both of our lives, but that he laid down the outline, the architectural model, for what future generations might encounter.'

Chase used the word *we*. As if they are all for one, all in this together. And yet. Mike rescans the face, with its wisps of patchy newborn hair trailing across the chin. It's the kind of hair that he recalls from adolescence, when he looked on each sign of the body's changing as a betrayal of some original, unspoken understanding.

Chase's small, precise hands fly across a sheet of paper, turning it into an origami cat that he settles next to the pair of dark flowers on the seat beside them. Whenever Marker was asked for a picture, he would send a photo of Guillaume-en-Égypte, his cat familiar. When he died, there were eight dead cats waiting in his freezer to be buried with him.

There is a warm flush of atoms in Mike's chest that only an hour ago was solid and impenetrable. The funeral mass, the burial of a French filmmaker – it's something that can't be managed alone, it requires company, some kind of collective seeing, like the cinema itself.

'Sometimes I wish I could have been one of his cats.' Mike offers it up with a note of apology.

'I know.'

'You mentioned that you had also...' Mike's hand waves in the air, conjuring unseen geometries. He wants to put away the voice that is working overtime to create boundaries and distances. There is something in this new stranger's force field that says: you are okay here. Chase thrives on unexpected intimacies. Here, in this faraway port, there is no future he couldn't contemplate. At least for a minute or two.

'You said that you also had an address in the second life,' Mike says, trying again.

'Yes.'

'But you don't look positive, forgive me for saying.'

'Nothing to forgive.' And then something in that smooth wall of a face gives way, as if Chase has grown suddenly tired of having to hold it up for so long. The words begin to pour out in no particular order, in an unrehearsed rush.

What might Chase say to summarize multiple decades of gender transgression in a few short lines that would require very little follow-up and/or additional explanation? 'The last time my sister was in town, she casually mentioned that she was the only one in our family who decided to keep her boobs and her birth name. Cute, eh?'

The announcement of delayed departures. The metallic clatter of motorized carts bearing the elderly across the endless real estate of the departure lounge. Mike imagines the aerial view; like Chase, he is also a filmmaker, and like Marker, he is also prolific, and he enjoys nothing more than composing shots, massaging distances, as if through a lens. The two heads leaning in close enough to touch. Newly disclosed trans meets positive, isolated realities now worth sharing. The sun casts long shadows across the oblong windows, so that everyone who passes by looks a thousand feet tall. It is the hour of giants, and they step into it together, lonely yet curious, newly unrehearsed.

They stand up at the same time, part of the same choreography, the seventh-inning stretch. Chase has a plane to catch in less than an hour that will return him to his familiars in Chicago. As they stroll toward his gate, a thought strikes him.

Chase: 'The modern novel began a couple of centuries ago as a collection of letters. It was a hybrid form that could throw its arms around a private correspondence, and more importantly, the private life that this correspondence made possible, and then recreate it as a feature of public life. The novel was a new kind of technology, and the long hours required to absorb it would help create the very interiority it was trying to describe. It seems the only way to have a private life was to bring it into the public.' It is a lie, but also a truth.

They arrive at the faraway gate where bored excitement adrenalizes the scrum. Joining the steadily growing queue, they realize it won't be long now. Chase glances at his fellow ghost detective and continues. The weird thing is, when Chase talks, it's as if the words are coming out of both their mouths at the same time. He is talking about the second life.

'I think we can both remember our first lives, the way we used to fall in love, the fearful list of thrills that we embraced for the first time. And then those lives stopped, and the stories that used to be the reason to get up every morning, they stopped too. I remember going to see yet another doctor, her desk crammed with script pads and samples, and her leaning across the piles to assure me: *You only live twice.*

'Today we're back from the dead, or at least, back from the lives we used to have. Only I have two bodies now, the one that gathers sensations and the other one that archives the records. Is it too terrible to admit that I prefer the record, that I find it more reassuring, even more erotic? Isn't that why both of us have spent too many hours combing through Mr. Marker's archives?'

At last Chase is finished with his pitch, ready to pose the question that lay hovering between them since they first made contact. Or was there a glimmer that shone even before that hope arrived?

'Why don't we work on something together?' Chase asks.

'Yes.'

'You haven't heard what I'm proposing.'

'Sure, I've heard.'

'Why don't we write a book of letters, a novel, that will make the second life possible?'

'Together?'

'Call it an alternating current. I'll send you something, and you can write back when the mood strikes.'

'You mean, the way the invention of the novel made the first life possible?'

'Yeah, we'll reboot the technology in three parts: first life, transition, second life.'

Chase offers a half-smile again and then he steps back into the swarm that is beginning to shuffle toward the robot voices at the counter. The sound of routinized cheer, the scrape of plastic wheels on tile. Scanners blink, a corporate clone ensures that everyone looks like their passport picture. Mike watches his new best friend grow smaller in the crush; soon it will be his turn to leave Orly, to wave Mr. Marker and his conjuring of the second life goodbye.

With a startling suddenness that could not be separated from violence, they could hardly wait to get started.

Chase

I'm writing you now from an underheated Chinatown walk-up that feels like it could make an appearance in Mr. Marker's *Remembrance of Things to Come*. I keep thinking about the differences between keeping a diary and sending a letter. They never found Marker's diaries – maybe they were just rumours after all – but he was a prolific letter writer, as I don't need to tell you.

I am an hour early for a date that is not a date. It is not a date because she is, admittedly, unavailable. But it is a date because we want it to be, non-admittedly. I'm always early for everything. If I added up the 'early time' I spend walking in loops around my destination, I would gain multiple days of living. Tonight, my destination is in Tribeca and my early walking affords opportunities to obsessively fidget with the collar of my leather jacket in any reflecting surface.

As I approach the restaurant, I can see that she is sitting in the window. The jury is out as to who I'd rather be in this scene: the one waiting at the table or the one who gets to walk in on time and casually say hello. I know it's a date because she looks stunning, she's not on her phone and she's already ordered a drink. As soon as I sit down, we start talking about the weather – nothing says nerves quite like 'Can you believe the day we are having?'

First dates are excellent vehicles for my best-self story-telling. I can slide polished anecdotes – which often tidily wrap up cumbersome histories – into the landscape of getting-to-know-you conversations with ease. But something about this is different – I have the kind of adrenaline in my throat that makes me want to barf or scream. Why is it that new crushes make me question all the skills I've spent my whole life refining? Of course it's not all crushes, just the ones that make me want to forget all of my old stories and start rewriting. When her face lifts to meet mine, I wonder: do you want to step into this second life with me?

Mike

The dizzying hope of your meet-up makes me want to jump into her body and say yes to you. How well I remember sitting at the window of Tank Noodle waiting on a computer date, though my not-yet-beloved's uploaded face was obscured with arty lighting so it was hard to tell what they looked like exactly. Everyone who stepped into the joint could be the one, and as each crossed the threshold I began to imagine our life together, or at least the opening lines, the first touch. The door hadn't been greased for a spell, so there was a distinct clamour of metal on metal that announced the arrival of each new hopeful.

Alex arrived fashionably late on a set of crutches – it was a biking accident, she said, though ten minutes later it was a bad fall in a quarry north of the city. She had a face that could walk through fire without showing the marks; she was stoned and effervescent and it became clear, after the noodles arrived, that she had never eaten Vietnamese soup and wasn't going to begin now. Eating was optional. We walked back to her apartment where she chain-smoked heaters (*Are you sure you don't want a hit?*) and all the words I ever knew flew south for the winter. She told me about the three guys she was seeing, the most menacing of which she called Boston, who was some kind of biker enforcer, and if he ever found out about the other two… I nodded sympathetically. I sat on the couch sympathetically. I fixed her drinks and emptied the ashtrays and changed records and then I told her I loved her and she laughed and then I laughed too and then she showed me to the door and I never saw her again.

Chase

I once walked in on my parents having sex, which was a remarkable feat as I'd only ever seen them kiss a handful of times. I was eight, it was Mother's Day, and I had gone downstairs early to make coffee. I'm not sure how I did that exactly, but after a successful brew, I tiptoed up the carpeted stairs to their bedroom and carefully opened the lever handle with my elbow, hoping to surprise them with my two cups of joe. Rounding the corner toward the bed, I saw them on top of each other, not really moving, and making little to no sound. Startled – but also as if I had rehearsed for this moment my entire life – I turned around quietly and pulled the door closed again behind my back. My next step? To set the coffee cups down on the floor, take a deep breath, knock on the door, pick up the cups and enter the room again. Of course, after the knock, they had taken up positions on opposite sides of the bed, probably never to have sex again.

A few years later, a friend told me about a public-access radio program called *Sunday Night Sex Show* with Sue Johanson wherein people would call to ask for sex advice. The show was awkwardly timed, six to eight p.m., which was earlier than my bedtime, and I was not one to go to bed before I had to. Successfully faking a stomachache one night, I huddled into bed eager for a secret listen. Unfortunately, the cord of my earphones wasn't long enough to allow me to remain settled on my pillow, so I had to spin around and put my head where my feet would be normally. Halfway through the show, my mom walked into my room to check on me. Startled by her entrance, I jolted up, pulling the headphones cleanly out of the stereo jack. 'AND THEN YOU CAN EASE THE PENIS INTO THE VAGINA,' replied Sue to a curious caller. 'My stomach is feeling better!' I said.

I think you're telling me: the first life is driven by the thing I never saw and that I can't help seeing over and over again. The radio voices of strangers allow me to restage the primal scene with my mother, not in the world of touch – that belongs to me alone – but as a shared description. If I've successfully come between you and Dad, then let's wait here together, while the national broadcast flows over the both of us and Sue Johanson takes us home one more time. Who needs penis in vagina when I can have your words in my mouth? Here in the second life, we have abandoned the project of making children and are dedicated to asking this question instead: what else could we make together?

Chase

I am in a Montreal hotel room sharing pillow space with a stunning blonde. We are talking about sex, casually oscillating between stories about the past and desires for the future in an effort to assess our compatibility – only people who are trying to sleep together talk about sex this much. I need to tell her why sex with me will be different from sex she has with other men, but even that statement feels tedious and annoying. Next time, I'm just going to wear a T-shirt that says, 'The product doesn't match the packaging.'

Mike

How to resist the allure of the surface? I wanted to marry my hypnotist until his talent for regression got the best of us both. I couldn't afford to see him more than a few times a year, a distance which added considerably to the erotic appeal. What could be sexier than not getting what you want? Dr. Henry asks me to concentrate on his eyes and begins counting down slowly from ten to one. Every time he says a number it is answered by a voice inside my head that says 'It's not going to work.' 'Nine.' 'It's not going to work.' 'Eight.' 'It's not going to work.' But as soon as he says, 'One,' a rigidity takes over my body. I am paralyzed in the chair, I am the chair. And still his voice is calling me, 'You are ten years old, lying in bed on Aberdeen Crescent. A faint breeze arrives from the open window.' And then I am no longer hearing his words, I am there again, feeling the flannel rub of pajamas against my elbows as I move from one side of the bed to the other. I am somewhere between asleep and awake when the sliver of light that runs across the bottom of the bedroom door suddenly widens and a figure appears in the doorway. I can see without seeing that it's my mother and close my eyes immediately. My heart pounds and I fold my body in on itself. I want to see what my brother is doing on the other side of the room, I want to communicate with him, but I don't know how. I know what I'm supposed to do because I've been trained to see myself, like Baudelaire's dandy, through the eyes of someone else. I learned how to act by becoming an actor, and if I wasn't able to secure the lead role in my life, that was only because it was occupied before I was conceived. I pretend to sleep and then I pretend to partially wake up. I look over at my brother and try to pass the cues over to him, but it's hard without words. He has a startled look on his face, the soft features a mask of fear because he can tell from my wound-up expressions that there's something he's supposed to know, but he doesn't know what it is. So he lets it pass.

My brother – his name is Johnson, like the old president (though it should really be Doormat, or Kick Me, to make things perfectly clear) – stumbles out into the living room. This is the living room, the rest of the house is the dying room. My father is there and I nearly jump out of the chair I have become as he turns to me, or at least in the general direction of me. This is my dad without the haze of Alzheimer's and too much daytime television. This is the father who still has a brain to lose. I have separated myself from Doormat, from my brother, because I'm worried he's going to get us into trouble. I'm not sure what we're doing out here yet – I can't tell whether my mother is angry or excited or both.

There is a live wire running through everybody here, as if a clumsy electrician had run an unshielded cable between family members. I can feel their blood inside my blood, I can hear the chromosomes dividing. The response of being so close to these bodies is so overwhelming, there are moments I can hardly feel anything at all. But it's obvious beyond mention that my feelings are not entirely my feelings. There is an orange ball of fear that keeps jumping out of my mother's forehead, like a headlamp, and underneath that there is a deep horizon of oil slick, black on black, which is where she keeps all the bodies from the internment camps during the Second World War. When the Japanese came and invaded her island universe they took everything away, and they've never stopped taking it away. The bodies she saw, the corpses lying in piles at the side of the road, never stopped bleeding. Not for one day. The invasion never ended, I know, because I have it right here, stored deep in my body, and it is more real to me in this moment, in this living room, than anything I have ever experienced. My deepest memories are not my memories. It's not that unusual, actually. But the way these memories are transmitted – could we call it my inheritance? – is something we might name as affect.

Let's return to the scene, shall we? But we'll rename the characters. So there is Doormat, that's my brother. There's God, that's my mother, and my dad the Holy Ghost. I'm Shithead. Doormat says, 'I wish I could be an astronaut,' because he wants to fit in, but the more he licks God's ass, the more likely his will get kicked. The Holy Ghost says, 'You'll have to wait until after your birthday,' and everybody laughs because the atmosphere is so tight we could do jumping jacks off it. I look down at my hand which is clenched up into a ball and tell it to relax, but my fingers can't speak the language. It seems the beginnings of a vast and unnameable fear has been successfully transmitted. It has jumped from human to human, blood to blood.

If I were to take a photograph of this moment, we might appear just like a family, but only because cameras aren't yet sensitive enough to show affect. In the future, the banal details will be omitted, and these scenes will show only vibrations and light, every instant that is not terror or trembling excitement will be scrubbed away so that we can enter the past more faithfully. God looks at Doormat, who as usual is looking in the wrong direction, meaning, not at God. I follow God's look to the hazy black-and-white screen as a figure climbs down a ladder in a very fine-looking suit that I would like to wear for the rest of my life, and there is a white-noise crackle coming out of the speakers, as if we are jacked in to his cerebral cortex. Actually, I don't think 'cerebral cortex,' I think, I can hear what he's hearing, Houston Control is in my head too. And this suit is designed, like the suit of the dandy, to ensure that the one wearing it doesn't feel anything at all. It carries the atmosphere of Houston, a pervasive, omnipresent state that allows me to live. I can live in this moon of a living room, so long as I don't feel anything and my lines are already scripted. 'One small step for Shithead, one giant leap,' etc. Even the *hahaha* I hear Neil Armstrong pour into the white noise the next day sounds like he's reading it off the giant teleprompter in the sky. He's been watched by Houston so long he's absorbed the look, he's absorbed the atmosphere, the feeling, of being watched. The steady hum of external surveillance has become internal surveillance. Where do my feelings stop and the emotions of my spacesuit begin?

The astronauts depart, but not before leaving behind 36,000 pounds of garbage. Thanks for the memories. Doormat wants to go to sleep and the Holy Ghost is eating walnuts that he's told us will expand in our stomachs and burst like hand grenades, which is his friendly way of saying: keep your little fucking hands off my nuts. I am worried that he will burst because he eats them compulsively, sometimes without even bothering to chew. Is this what the Holy Ghost spends his time at night doing? It looks like he's taken it up as a kind of second job, and that makes me worried that I'm not working, only unlike God, he doesn't live inside me. He lives outside the perimeter, outside the Zone. I snap out of my trance. Somewhere God is smiling, the Holy Ghost is nodding and Doormat is saying yes. It was our first moon landing together. Shithead says, *Houston, I'm coming home.*

Chase

In the sixty-one movies listed in the IMDb database attributed to Chris Marker, there is not a single kiss. Though as we both know, there remains an explosive archival spread that WikiLeaks has promised to release that will recreate Marker's real-time web browsings from the past two decades. Perhaps there are kisses waiting to be uncovered there, though maybe kissing doesn't live easily in documentary; perhaps it is too tender or too cruel to be rendered as anything but fiction.

Kissing is one of life's most refined and tender skills, only refined and tenderized through trial and error. My first kiss transpired under the belly of a black grand piano in the basement of my friend Corey's house. His mom was upstairs cooking, and we were downstairs playing hide-and-go-seek. I saw a picture of Corey recently, and he remains a spitting image of his childhood face. I wonder what he would say of me?

My first prolonged, horizontal, make-out session also materialized in a basement, and came as the result of winning or losing a ping-pong game. I can't remember the rules exactly, but any way you played it, you wound up on the couch kissing.

Cinema's first kiss was filmed by Thomas Edison in 1896. We are presented with an apparently well-to-do couple sharing a quick peck in a proto-porn moment. She seems less than enthused by the idea – it's hard not to feel the coercion, the myth of progress and the steep gender grade all this weight is being pulled across. But I can't help wondering whether my kisses are fiction or documentary. In my first life, when I was still a kissing inventor, when the world of kissing stretched out before me as a blank promise, was I already filling in the holes with stories? Already becoming someone else?

There was a time in my life when I had more experience kissing people who had facial hair than I did kissing others through lip fuzz of my own. 'Tis a strange flip of the sensorial switch, and while I love the aesthetics of a well-manicured five-o'clock shadow – who am I kidding, that shadow growth takes me approximately two weeks – I do feel inhibited. I genuinely want to know, does Tom Selleck feel *anything* when he kisses people?

Mike

'Why don't you kiss and make up?' Isn't that how every childhood spat was supposed to be resolved? Sealed with a kiss. It's as if, as you suggest, kissing is already fiction, already a form of making it up, along with every form of intimacy I like to name as my own.

Your smooching reflection reminds me of the only joke I've ever been able to remember. It's from an old TV show called *The Flying Nun*. Two sisters, or perhaps they are sisters in training, are smoking in the basement when the innocent heroine chances upon them. 'Why are you smoking?' she asks, as if addiction were a question that can be answered. Both sisters look back at her, the pretty one and the other one who does all the talking. 'So we have something to give up for Lent.' I chuckled along with the canned laughter without actually knowing what Lent was. But reading your words makes me want to kiss someone again, so that I can have the pleasure of giving up kissing.

Let me return to the couch of my childhood for another TV moment. I am watching *Star Trek* and my mother is close enough to count every vein, though she has no use for a future that appears as designer escapism. Kirk and Spock are imprisoned on a forbidden planet, and as they battle the irrationality of their captors, Spock loses his shirt, though his look of bemused curiosity never wavers.

What did she say then, the source of all language and understanding? Mother: 'Well, I see he has at least one redeeming feature.' How confusing it was to be met by an overt expression of my mother's sexuality, especially because it was projected on to the half-human who was supposed to have left his body behind. My contract with masculinity began here, with Spock's perfect chest, which I saw through the eyes of my mother. How could I ever be a man if I wasn't first a woman, looking out from her eyes, seeing as she saw, nodding in time? I was jolted awake into a sudden and uncomfortable recognition, though I had no idea what was coming into focus. I felt sick to my stomach, or perhaps I was sick to her stomach. I wanted to leave the room immediately, but of course I did nothing. I sat paralyzed, and that became the second lesson about the operation of desire. Let's take it again from the top, repeat after me: double vision, recognition, arousal, paralysis. Or to put it in the words of the show's creator: to go where no man has gone before.

Chase

Before my mom converted to Orthodox Judaism, our family spent each Boxing Day in the suburbs with family and friends. The celebration always had two distinct yet compatible parts: presents and party. Though that division might also be summarized as: kids eating meatballs and adults getting drunk. Boxing Day was single-handedly responsible for introducing me to euchre, darts and the gastrointestinal distress caused by Bailey's Irish Cream.

In the mid-nineties, the host took it upon himself to refinish the basement as a den of masculine wonders. The pool table, wet bar, wine cellar, tool room, ugly couches, plyboard walls and corresponding sensibility became the organizing principle of Boxing Day parties thereafter. After dinner, the men would retreat to the basement for the remainder of the evening to play pool and drink beer, while the women would sit upstairs cleaning and drinking tea. It was a predictable patriarchy.

Of course, I always went with the men – a fact that no one seemed to notice or care much about. I hung out with the men not necessarily because I liked them better, but because I liked what they were doing. How many rails can the white ball hit before knocking the yellow-stripe into the corner pocket? How early do I have to get downstairs in order to secure the darts with the Canadian-flag flights rather than the Union Jacks? Like clockwork, my mom would peek her head downstairs at midnight to announce that it was time to go home, and I would kick a fit because I was not yet done trying to win whatever game we were playing.

One year, while putting on our coats and boots, a partygoer approached me with wet lips poised for a goodbye kiss. Something in my mom snapped. We left the party quickly and she burst into tears as we shut the doors of the car. 'DON'T YOU EVER LET THAT MAN GET THAT CLOSE TO YOU AGAIN!' she screamed. 'What the heck is your problem, Mom? It was seriously no big deal...' I said.

What I meant was 'I can handle everything.' 'It's no big deal' is a placeholder for 'Don't be sad' and 'I will try to make this go away.' Of course I can't make anything go away – her past, my past, our pasts, they are imprinted like footprints in wet concrete, forever available to those who'd like to find and seek.

When she was eight, my mom was abused by a group of young boys, and the ringleader was that man, the seeker of the Boxing Day wet kiss. I didn't know that at the time. To me, he was just an insurance adjuster from a small town, with an uninspired mustache that hadn't changed in my lifetime.

My mom is a master of keeping up appearances, a skill now further refined by the protective trappings of Orthodox Judaism. To be a good mother is to allow your kids to see their cousins at Christmas. To be a good daughter is to purchase gifts for your frigid mother. To be a good sister is to never talk about all that has happened. Period.

Chase

I loved visiting my dad at work. As the president of a large consumer electronics company, he had the biggest office in the building, and a penholder that doubled as a giant tarantula case; it was equal parts cool and disgusting. My visits were always the same. Upon arrival, I would politely say hello to all of his co-workers, and then run directly back to the warehouse. There were the men responsible for the company's import/export business, a task that required the continuous use of colossal forklifts, Styrofoam-peanut machines and giant rolls of packing tape. At lunch, I would rejoin my dad in the room adjacent to his office, and we would watch laserdiscs of live concerts together. It was long into adulthood before I realized that he didn't really like Barbra Streisand or Phil Collins and was only playing them for me. Years later, we would find common ground in Miles Davis and Thelonius Monk. Their sonic influence remains our longest-standing agreement.

I wasn't really working during those days in the warehouse – I was small, the jobs were big, and everyone was humouring me. That said, I was granted one warehouse object of my choosing as payment for each visit, and thus spent the majority of my time investigating potentially take-home-worthy headphones and CD players. When not scavenging for my reward, I could be found in the ripped, dusty swivel chair next to Fred. Fred was the boss of the warehouse and wore a blue one-piece mechanic's jumpsuit that had his name on it. He had daughters too, but he was good at reminding me that I was nothing like them.

All of the men that worked in the warehouse were filthy, a notable observation because the warehouse itself was beyond clean. Ripped T-shirts, mud-caked shoes and ratty hair were warehouse style priorities. 'We wouldn't be able to get anything done back here if we had to wear suits!' said Fred as he hoisted me up onto the speaker boxes. 'Why do you think everyone is so afraid of getting dirty?'

My dad was never dirty – a fact that reinforced my understanding that the cleanest people are often capable of making the biggest mess.

Mike

Marcel Duchamp wrote, 'A guest plus a host equals a ghost.' I was never all that good at equations, but my father was, when he wasn't busy turning into the background. He was a ghostly presence in my formative years, like a piece of benevolent furniture. He managed to avoid most paternal functions with his easygoing distractions, but the day finally came when I had to learn what were then called, without a shade of irony, 'the facts of life.' Facts were in short supply in the days before Wikipedia, so the whole thing could be summarized in a brief lecture that my father related in a sort of joke. He said that back in his native Indonesia, three men were determined to break the social code of their poverty and achieve respectability and success. Their beautiful social-engineering plans required capital, so they decided to rob the city's largest bank. After months of planning, they undertook the robbery, digging elaborate tunnels and drilling into the vault. Imagine their surprise when all they found were tubs of yogurt. Vowing revenge, they ate the yogurt and sealed up their perfect tunnels. The following morning all the local papers carried the same lead: *Unexplained robbery at sperm bank.*

Chase

In the early nineties, my dad and I won five out of the five father-daughter golf tournaments that we entered. Our streak resulted in extensive bragging, a collection of paperweight-shaped crystal trophies, and our names listed permanently on the clubhouse champion wall. Winning these tournaments was really quite easy, mostly because very few fathers had daughters who wanted to play with them, but also because we were good. We weren't good in the athletic prowess sense, but in the more all-encompassing golfing enterprise of rapport, flair and personality.

I started golfing with my dad long before I could hold a club. In Florida, he used to let my friend Josh and me drive the cart – the result was that he can now tell a story about how two seven-year-olds ran over his foot while barrelling down a hill. Golf was the perfect activity for extended homo-social bonding – homosocial in this context meaning men and me. As there was not a lot of action in the sport, there was ample time for talking and drinking.

Around eleven I started to forgo my closet in favour of my dad's clothes, and by seventeen I had stopped golfing completely. It wasn't that I hated the activity, but rather that after Dad left our family, I became interested in other things. To this day, he remains a member of the same club, and our reputation as winners persists. He is often asked, 'Where is your daughter these days? Do you two still play together?' His response? 'No, not anymore. She moved to California!'

Mike

I wonder what kind of second life his ghost daughter is leading in California and how many other people he has banished there. Do we all have Californias where we are busy putting our unspeakable pasts? How very fortunate that we've taken up this secret public writing between us, so that I can tell you about the self models I've left behind and open a few of the closets that I've constructed the better part of my nature from. Could you be my alibi, my cover story and my beard? Of course the favours would be mutual – I'd like to offer you the same emotional service station. Perhaps we could call the mementoes passed between us simply *California*.

Chase

Telling stories with you allows me to imagine new pathways; this is a road now travelled together. Have you become my second-life story incubator? The holder of my secrets, many too old and now some too new to otherwise properly articulate? My mom tells the same stories over and over again. I used to think it was because she was getting older, but I now understand her rehearsed narrations as a form of self-protection. If the story never changes, then ambiguity and revision are always kept at bay. I catch myself miming her conversational patterns on occasion – telling a story that is so refined and structured that it could be about anyone, anywhere. I think my mom and I both recognize that our stories are no longer true in the way that we tell them, but we rely on our scripts anyway. Perhaps we are rehearsing, or perhaps we are building a safe house with a sign on the door that reads 'All versions are fine here,' with a host who answers the door saying, 'I will love you anyway.'

It's strange, yet so familiar, to be writing to you in this way. In part, because I was watching your movies so long before I met you; the versions of you in public that I have now internalized privately. Movies like yours make movies like mine feel possible. Thanks for asking to see *Akin*. I always knew that I'd make a film about my mother. Partly because the collision of my transition and her conversion to Orthodox Judaism were so similarly and therefore excellently timed, and partly because there was so much worth exploring beyond the scope of our two tabloid-worthy histories.

When we drove past the hospital, I remember thinking it was some kind of fucked-up poetry that you were so sick while you were supposedly building your dream. That the time of our greatest wealth was also the time of our greatest suffering. We don't talk about it much anymore. About when you went away to recover from past violence, and that while you were gone the same violence found me. I know that when you were a kid, there was no way of escaping, but when it happened to me, you packed up our things. (from *Akin*)

'I don't know what I'm doing yet,' I said to her as I suggested we go back to our old town together. 'If you wouldn't mind driving, I'm just going to start shooting.' And it was true, partly. I didn't know what I was doing, but I did know what I was thinking. The result of our time together was three hours of shakily shot out-the-window-of-a-moving-car footage, and a suffocating silence. When I asked if she'd ever return to live in the town again, she responded, 'Nope. It's not who I am. I'm not sure who I am, but I'm not this. And it wasn't who I was then, either.' Perhaps a follow-up question to that statement was required, but I couldn't find it.

When I first started transitioning, and we'd encounter people who continued to refer to me with female pronouns, you would always say, 'Don't worry about it, it's just because you have such pretty eyes.' Your response always made me smile, as anyone who has ever seen us knows that I have your eyes. Therefore, in your defence of me there was a compliment of you. The strength of our family is rooted in the survival of women, one of them being you and one of them being me. It's a history now kept secret, under the veils of religious modesty and the illusions of a gendered dream. I want you to know that I remember, that I look to you often as a way to find me.

The truth is, people don't know anything when they see us. When they see a mother and a son, this version of you, alongside this version of me. The truth of our story is found in the moments when your wig comes off. And the scars on my chest are finally seen. This town is just a casing, a frame of a picture that is no longer. Today we became its visitors, reflecting back upon it a past that only you and I can see. (from *Akin*)

During the only occasion that we parked the car that afternoon, my mom exclaimed, 'It's another life. Yes, it impacts you, but don't go back to it because it keeps you stuck back there instead of moving forward.' And that was it; there was no other conversation.

Mike

After your drive, you sat down and scribbled out your life as if it were a script, as if all those experiences could be laid down in a line that even strangers could follow. It's a marvel how you can say so much and still hold something back for yourself and your mother. It's a movie that keeps its wig on. Please forgive me for asking again, but you've led me to a door that declares, 'Here are my secrets, no trespassing!' so it's difficult not to knock. I wonder if you could talk about what happened when your mother went to the hospital to recover her lost memories. You say, 'While you were gone, the same violence found me.' The presumption is that you are speaking about your father, though perhaps you're nodding toward another source of distress.

Chase

The presumption isn't right. My dad is all over the project precisely because he is so absent from the story, but when my mom left, he was gone too. Physically and emotionally.

I often think about the stories I won't tell, or the details I avoid in service of better focus and cleaner narration, even while the concealed specificities remain the foundation upon which my storytelling strategies sit. Sexual violence can take things away: control, power, consent and safety. For me, part of living now is an active redistribution of that power play, by managing the boundaries of what I give and what I take. Showing work in public ensures that such processes of disclosure are always at my discretion.

Nothing can be stolen if you consent to give it away.

Mike

When I first became HIV-positive, I struggled to find a way to tell my friends. Never mind the talking cure, this was the untalking cure. When we were both thoroughly lubricated, I laid it out for my best pal, Darren, who promptly sat down like I'd put an anvil in his pants. He didn't say anything for the longest thirty seconds in human history, and then his face wound up in a rictus of pain. 'What does that even mean?' he asked in the voice of a six-year-old. I wanted to be six years old too, but there was another part that had to be played first. I tried to lay out the mechanics so that I could stop feeling his feelings, but the viral progressions weren't so clear yet – it would be many years before science would conjure its miracle cures. I felt bad for making him feel so awful – obviously I had let him down, and I wondered for the first time whether we would still be friends after we stepped out the door. It turns out I needn't have worried on that score, but as the weeks went on and I grew reluctant to repeat the disappointment machine, Darren kept after me to share the load. Not being able to talk to people about it gave him migraines. He said it was like being gifted a lit bomb that he was forced to watch every day in the middle of his living room. And you think you've got problems? Though as the weeks turned into months, and I blew past even the most soft-headed and deliriously optimistic forecasts, dying became the new normal, and we could return to smaller and more routine disappointments. Along with undreamt pleasures.

I hadn't realized how this single infection would spread across the landscape of my friends, changing everything. The fear that I had held close all my life, reliable companion, the friendship before friendship, was justified after all. You were right all along! Making movies became a way to have a more creative relationship with my fear. As you said to me once, art-making was a way of 'visually reorganizing my shame.'

I can also feel fear in your work, along with the need to massage that fear into public forms. It's a form of *mede-cine*, a healing that isn't confined to you alone. I could imagine, before each of your autobiographical movies, a shot of a man running at night with a superimposed title that reads: *This is a film about you. Not its maker.*

Chase

If you stop using a path, it grows over, reclaimed by forest. They seem perpetually linked; as the path, the next step, is always guided in some capacity by an original wounding, isn't it?

It was 1989. I was enrolled in an arts-based summer camp, which offered a variety of busy-making workshops and personal hideaways. On the final day, parents were invited to join their children for an official show-and-tell of the session's work. 'Your son was such a pleasure to have at camp,' said the counsellor as she helped load popsicle-stick projects into the trunk of the car. 'You mean my daughter?' inquired my mom. 'No, your… son?' I jumped in the back seat and shut the door, avoiding eye contact with everybody.

The next summer, my parents managed to get me on an all-boys baseball team, as I was bored of arts and crafts and temporarily unenthused by the prospect of soccer. Thankfully, at ten years old, everybody looks and sounds the same in sock stirrups and a snapback.

After one notable Little League win, my teammates assembled on the dugout bench, legs spread wide and hands in fists. 'Come sit down, we're celebrating!' they yelled. As I approached, each boy started rhythmically rapping his knuckles on his jock cup to the beat of our team cheer.

'Oh, I'm sorry, I think my dad is here to pick me up...' I said, cup-less.

The next morning, I asked my dad to drive to National Sports so that I could ask about jockstraps for girls. The sales associate introduced us to a product named 'The Jill,' which could be summarized as nothing more than a triangular piece of flat plastic with dangling elastic straps. 'This is the dumbest thing I have ever seen,' I said loudly, and asked for a jock instead. The cup cut into the creases of my legs when I walked, but I internalized the sting as penance for feeling like such a badass. There is a price one must pay for strategic invisibility.

Mike

How does the old adage rhyme? *There's many a slip 'twixt the cup and the lip.* Though that was coined at a moment when cups were filled with imperial tea booty, newly recoded as national pride, not the herd stomp that you declined, preferring the company of a different drummer. How can I feel the cheer of belonging without my cup? How is it possible to join a gender club, for instance, without refusing the other side? The first life feels caught between yes and no, male or female – either you're wearing a cup and you're on my team, or you're the enemy. The cold war, the steady drumbeat of the nation state. It's interesting to compare the borders of the original thirteen colonies with the rest of what would become the United States. The first borders follow landscape eruptions and rivers, while the new states in the west were drawn on paper in straight lines. They arrive from a terrifying distance, drafted by statesmen who had never set eyes on the territory. It can be hard to refuse state lessons in life drawing when it comes to marking up our own fields of belonging, especially when we're trapped inside our first life. The lines are so long, so seamlessly integrated into everyday life, that it can be hard to see them at all. Don't you find?

Sometimes I don't know where my lines are, until someone shows them to me. While in Manhattan this past October, I had brunch with my first girlfriend. The title of 'first' is always specific and striking to me, as it means that no one else can ever be identified that way. There is only one first kiss, there is only one first heartbreak, and there is only one first girlfriend. She arrived in my life at nineteen, when I was otherwise happily dating men. Like many young lovers, we lacked the necessary communication skills to foster an environment for a relationship worth keeping. Our breakup was abrupt, unresolved and heart-wrenching.

Fifteen years later, she lives on the Lower West Side with a boyfriend who looks like Matthew McConaughey, and a cross-eyed dog with an underbite. Aside from her new porcelain teeth, she looks and sounds the same. Believe me when I say that's a compliment, and that the teeth are beautiful but entirely unnecessary. The brunch started as all brunches do, with my silent judgment over the price of eggs and the accompanying impulse to order more than one $4 coffee. We talked about our siblings, our jobs and our love of champagne. Of course, the unspoken conversation that was happening in tandem to our small talk was that I had transitioned since last we met, and was sitting before her with facial hair, no chest and a new name.

After eating, we wandered the streets of the city and our conversation settled into a strangely familiar place. Was it old feelings or new ones that allowed us to meander in this way? Walking through Washington Square Park, we could have been on a date.

I wonder if young love lingers on account of our inability to put it away? It was so easy to walk beside her, looking at an older, more generous version of her face.

When I arrived home, our communication intensified, with questions of when and how we might see each other again bubbling to the surface 'It's always been this way...' she said in a note, to which I immediately responded, 'No it hasn't, my life has entirely changed...'

It became clear to me that she had stepped into a place we had never been before, and didn't have any need for the new borders I had so carefully laid. Could I join her in this crossing, or would I have to stay inside the carefully manicured walls I had so steadfastly built and maintained?

0.9
Love Letters

Mike

The first person I ever fell in love with was my cousin Mara. Sixteen years old, going on a hundred. Determined to grow old before her time. She looked like a cross between my mother and me; for a mercifully brief moment in my adolescence this constituted an ideal of beauty. Our difficulty was that we lived on different continents: she lived in Brasilia while I called the suburbs of Toronto home. She had arrived during a family visit so closely guarded that we might have spent all of half an hour by ourselves. Trying to keep anyone else in the over-crowded family rooms from noticing what was going on turned our faces into icy masks of boredom. I had never wanted to touch someone so much. I remember having to sit on my hands so they would stop shaking, while trying to keep the rest of my body very still. I breathed into muscle after muscle, asking each one to relax, until I wasn't expressing an ounce of preference. I was certain that the moment we dropped our Swiss flags of emotional neutrality that she would be taken away and we would never see each other again. A few days later she was gone.

After she left, we began writing letters to each other, filling pages with extravagant promises we had no way of keeping. I didn't realize then how much I longed for the distance that separated us, and I confused us both by writing her about how I longed for her instead. She was a willing partner in the deception, of course – we were strangers to each other, so how could she know otherwise?

We wrote each other nearly every day, so after a stomach-turning delay that was so painful I fell into bed with a high fever, there began to arrive a steady flow of correspondence, sometimes two or three in an afternoon. There was something out of focus about my life before these letters, as if I had never quite broken through the fetal membrane. I had been an indifferent student, easily distracted, but now there were letters filled with quick-witted observations and canny asides. Perhaps I would never be a real person, but I could write about one. Novels helped. I copied out a passage on seal rescue from Peter Singer, and when Mara wrote me back in her breathless schoolgirl prose asking if I had really rescued a seal, I admitted that it was my brother who had managed the feat.

In a stroke of terrible cruelty, the Canadian post office undertook its lengthiest and most bitter strike at this moment. There was a marked wage division between inside and outside workers, and the two unions were determined to balance the scales. After five months, the government caved – public pressure was simply too much to endure, but by then, despite a rash of telegrams, our first and most perfect affair was over.

Chase

My favourite Chris Marker film remains *Sans Soleil* (*Sunless*), though it's hard to imagine it summoning global audiences today. It's a wandering and philosophical love letter written to a woman we never meet, by a man who remains mysterious. There are heart-stopping passages about hunger and dreams. But it is the exchange of letters, or the failure of exchange, that quickens the pulse. Like the affair you describe, it is distance that brings these lovers together.

My sister Sarah and I have been charged by our mother with the task of organizing a giant trove of family photos. Only one container of photos remains in our family – it has been long left unattended, and it is haphazardly overflowing. From its inception, we understood the task to be less about organization and more about emotional eradication. If the photos were to remain in our lives, they were to remain out of our mom's house, elsewhere.

Elsewhere is now with me.

'We need some organizational categories,' said Sarah as she looked across the scattered piles of negatives, yellowing album pages and bent Polaroids. 'You, me, Mom and Dad, other family, oversized prints, random objects, and a pile for people we can't identify.'

At first the sorting was easy. I was excited to be able to tell Sarah that the human in all of the photos with a head shaped like a potato was in fact her as a baby. Apparently she had been carrying around the quietly depressing assumption that she had been photographically neglected all these years. The revelation inspired visible relief. Nobody has ever re-encountered a version of their face more lovingly.

Of course, like many necessary familial excavations, what was easy and light became unbearable; this occurred exactly at the moment we found photos of people we never wanted to see again. It was amazing to think that they had been living alongside us in this bin for so long, waiting to be rediscovered. Re-recognized. Re-acknowledged. Little wonder that my mom finally kicked them out.

Mike

My brother Johnson is behind me, pushing - he's even starting to break out into a little run though I know he's not big on running. He hates breaking into a sweat because he's worried about losing his body fluids, which he imagines like oil or bauxite, precious metals that have to be conserved. Johnson's my younger brother, so maybe it's weird that he's teaching me how to ride a bike, but he couldn't wait to swap his legs for wheels, just like he couldn't wait to learn how to breathe out the first notes on the harmonica we passed between us on those nights before black-and-white television became colour television and there was suddenly no more room for homemade soundtracks. I am really flying along now on a bicycle that mysteriously appeared behind our house just last weekend, its worn plastic grips slippery to the touch and only slightly out of reach. He is propelling me forward as I struggle to regain purchase on a seat worn smooth from a hundred easy cruises, and then I can feel his hands release and I am hurtling toward the boulevard at the end of our driveway. I catch a glimpse of a red crimson blur at the edge of the visual field as it occurs to me that I don't know how to brake exactly - that was going to be covered in lesson two - so as the car jets across the smooth slope I throw myself off the bicycle machine and watch it clatter harmlessly against the Ford Seville's grille as a startled cowboy hurls curses in a foreign language and slams to a stop.

'You'll never do that again.' Are the words directed at me or the driver? Johnson approaches the scene channeling his inner forensics geek as the cowboy steps out of the vehicle to vent some serious spleen, pausing to caress the dent in his fender like a man in love. I'm missing some of the meatier parts of my calf, but he seems to be accusing me of trying to murder him using myself as a missile. Johnson walks over to the wounded bicycle wreck and picks it up the way he might lift a wounded puppy. He speaks to the man in a colourless tone that lets all of the air out of the afternoon, 'You nearly killed my brother,' and offers me a flick of the head. We're headed back inside.

My brother called them dress rehearsals. He said the most important show you'll ever make is your own death, something far too important to leave to chance. As a result, dress rehearsals were necessary, and we spent our childhoods crawling through the orchard at the end of the block, dying from malaria or snakebite. Or else shivering in deep winter, naked in the neighbour's shed, waiting for what we called the blue rainbow to streak across our skin. Or else we would clamber out to the abandoned quarry and jump from one of the rickety metal silo ladders into a scummy pothole. Breathless and shivering on the long walks home, I asked him if he was afraid to die. He started laughing then and couldn't stop until he held on to me and wheezed water out of his nose. 'Of course I'm scared – if I wasn't, it wouldn't be any kind of fun.' So why are we doing all this stuff, I wanted to ask him, though I didn't put it like that exactly, but rounded it off so it sounded more like encouraging words. But they weren't encouraging enough, I guess, because he shot me a look as if I had just landed from a distant planet before laying down a phrase I wouldn't hear until a couple more decades had passed. 'You only live twice.'

Today I feel like I'm back on that bike. Writing these words to you. Imagine my surprise when you invited me to walk across the landscape of your brand-new face one afternoon and see how you were also busy living a second life. Oh, you too! I never would have guessed. But then the whole point is that no one could possibly tell. Who am I, if I am not my cover story? The promise of our mutual discovery was that one day you would tell me how you managed to do reconstructive surgery on your storytelling machine. We all know the fairytales that sustain the first life. How does the fine print go again? Until death do us part. But now that we've survived the death of our former selves, how do we keep a new kind of hope alive when part of the cost of passage, part of the necessary toll-taking, was that we had to leave all the old hopes at the door? I guess I'm really asking: can you help me?

Chase

Here's James Baldwin in the most important book I've ever read about cinema and its impacts, *The Devil Finds Work*: 'A story is impelled by the necessity to reveal: the aim of the story is revelation, which means that a story can have nothing – at least not deliberately – to hide. This also means that a story resolves nothing. The resolution of a story must occur in us, with what we make of the questions which the story leaves us.'

I've been paying close attention to the ruptures in my storytelling machinery, past and present. While we might make valiant attempts to compartmentalize our fractured lives, I believe that all ruptures are related. My present-day sensemaking strategies are informed by the lack of sense found in my history.

I remember the first time that my mom introduced me to menstruation. 'You will notice that as your body starts changing...' she opened warmly. A nurse by trade, my mom's ability to talk about bodies and related functions is always measured and steady. I knew a little bit about menstruation. When I was nine, my neighbour Jessie and I stole tampons from my mom's bathroom and ran up to my room to investigate. Small, paper-wrapped, cardboard cylinders lay strewn across my bed. 'I know how to use these,' said Jessie confidently, as she ran into my closet only to reveal herself moments later, pantsless. When she re-emerged, the taut cotton was pressed gently, externally, between her legs. It looked like an undressed hotdog in a bun.

After a routine doctor's appointment in the fall of Grade 8, my mom stopped at the pharmacy to buy a box of tampons. When we got into the car, she opened the box and handed me the paper instructions. The writing was microscopic, and there was an anatomical drawing of a bisected body showing the pathway the tampon should take.

Seeing the image made me choke. Something about that diagram sucked all the air out of my lungs. I don't remember what, if anything, my mom said to me, but by the time I had stopped crying she had put the instructions away. It took me almost a decade to realize that the diagram revealed parts of my body that someone else had seen, and to understand that such seeing was never of my choosing.

'The resolution of a story must occur within us…' I think Baldwin is telling us that stories serve as pathways, but they are never routes with clear ends. According to Baldwin, only plots have conclusions, because plots provide answers to pretend questions. Knowing that the in points and out points of our self-understanding are never fixed means that our second lives may be no clearer than our firsts.

Transition

'I was wrong on all counts – imprisoned, as I was and still am, by my own hopes and fears. I'm not trying to fix that wrongness here, I'm just trying to let it *hang out*.'

– Maggie Nelson, *The Argonauts*

1.0
Festival

Mike and Chase attend a festival that presents the projection of a single film, Chris Marker's *La Jetée*, played one hundred times in succession, over a period of three days. Together, they emerge sleepless and exhilarated. After the first dozen repetitions had exhausted every narrative possibility, and the next dozen had flickered past offering the delights of beauty and composition, what they were left with was a clear blueprint for the second life. It was a voyage that each would have to take alone, but there was consolation in knowing that others had already cleared a way. It wasn't just about Marker anymore. It was about other trans people and those living with AIDS. Intersecting legacies, threads overlapping and tied together, deep.

Huddled together in Ten Belles café, just across the road from Marker's last apartment, they order Americanos and brioche. When Mike suggests they remain silent and pass notes to each other, Chase can't help laughing. There is a question that each is holding for the other, but they don't know the words for it yet. The brioche is still warm from the morning's oven. The caffeine nearly revives them. When they sit down to write there is always more to say, but now language refuses them. Exhaustion is written over every gesture – even lifting a spoon requires an effort of concentration. The round table, the round hands of a clock, their waiter's face. The half-moon cuticles of Chase's fingers as they wrap around the mug. The rings beneath Mike's eyes. Their respective planes are due to depart later that afternoon; as has become their custom, they will say goodbye in Orly.

1.1
Reveal

Mike

Sunday arrives without shadows, the paling sky clear as if there were no more secrets left to keep. Johnson and I peg the meeting for noon, inside an urban cavern that has been retroconverted into a bookstore. They encourage patrons to shell peanuts onto the floor, which tickles my brother and a few other book tourists, judging by the sedimented undergrowth that leads us to the back of the reading room. He's grown a beard to fill out his soft chin, and I offer appreciations that he bats away. We haven't seen each other in a year because he's on the road selling aluminum futures, or that's the story we prefer to tell. I think both of us are still trying to work out escape routes from the past, but as soon as we see each other we turn into the most unwanted versions of ourselves. He pulls the baseball hat lower and squints back at me, smiling.

'I missed you.'

'I missed you too, Johnson.'

'You know, after Roger moved out ... did you ever meet Roger?

'The big guy with the *It Takes a Union* tat up his sleeve?'

'Yeah, whatever. We were just bitching all the time so I told him he had to find somewhere else to park his bad feelings.'

'I'm sorry.'

'I'm not sorry – I started feeling again, you know? The way this table curves, the sun when it hits my face in the morning, as soon as Roger showed up my feelings took a powder.'

'Took a what?'

'A powder. It's an expression. I'm just trying to say that as soon as anyone shows up for me, and really wants to be with me, I don't know what I feel anymore.'

The two brothers look at each other and a grin spreads across them as if they were one face. Even sadness makes them happy.

'So what did you want to tell me?'

'Excuse me?'

'It's written all over your face, you want to tell me something, and you even let me pick the place, figuring it would make me feel more comfortable. For you to surrender that kind of control must mean it's a big news item.'

He was the first one I told I was HIV-positive. I'd never seen him cry before, or at least not since he was five, and that was just because he caught his hand in the door. When we held each other and whispered *I love you*s, I knew why it had taken so long to tell him. My sickness was real now, because it lived independently of me. From now on, it would live in my brother as a reminder that we would never be young again, never young enough to change what had already happened. Before we spoke, my illness was a professional concern discussed with the doctor, drawn up in charts and tables. If my body had become a danger in my sexual relations, with Johnson it had become again a house, a place where blood was thicker than the years we'd grown apart, a place where the certainty of death was no longer disguised by our youth.

Whenever we met, there was this special thing we would do which we always pretended we weren't doing. We practised saying goodbye. Every moment was the last moment, every hug was the finale – he was on shore waving while I was on the ship sailing to the last country in the world. And then the cocktail arrived and ruined our perfect ending, the one we had rehearsed since we began loading our memory banks. It seemed I was going to be granted a second life, and my brother was enlisted to play a new part; after all these years of secret admiration, he could take my place and enter a state of permanent illness and disability. In my second life, every one of my relationships underwent a drastic shift. There were many who preferred the dying version I performed and set off to find it elsewhere, while others undertook the role reversal my brother embraced. It was as if I had infected all of my friends, and now we all had to reassemble our broken parts in the funhouse mirrors of modern medicine.

Chase

For me, the turning point of transition was excruciatingly slow. When I finally resolved to come out, I remember wishing that I might wake up the next morning a towering hulk of a man, with the gritty details of my transformation already prepackaged into smoothly humorous sound bites. The reality, of course, is that transitioning begins as a brain game. Wait – for me, transitioning is *always* a brain game. But the levels of negotiation required to initiate the physical processes are varied and layered, from personal and emotional to procedural, financial and institutional.

A few days after I had started to tell people of my decision, I was sitting in a San Francisco park with a large group of friends. With various conversations happening simultaneously, I couldn't hear someone calling my name, and as a result everyone was laughing. I turned around to meet the speaker's eyes clearly. 'I was yelling *Chase! Chase!* But you couldn't hear your new name.' It was embarrassing, but I laughed because everyone else was laughing. The fantasy of revealing myself anew in public was replaced by the creeping acknowledgement that my past would never escape.

It was so very long after that day before anything physical would happen to my body related to transitioning. I continually looked to others for proof that life was possible, projecting on to them my hope and fears for an alternative embodied state.

For me, what emerges in the story about your brother is the story of you. It serves as a transplantation of affect and experience, of fear and projection. Your movies similarly craft your position through the positions of others, taking their personal intricacies and then mapping them out on to contexts far beyond themselves.

The first time I saw your short movie *Positiv* (1998), I didn't know you were positive. What continues to haunt me about that work is your full-frontal monologue of experience, which is so absent from your other makings. You place your face quite literally adjacent to, and in conversation with, images made by others, but you don't hide behind them. It makes me wonder if you might actually be able to see yourself more clearly through the veils and facades of other people?

Mike

I always feel I am quoting. I open my mouth and someone else's voice sings out the tune. You don't find? The closer I get to the unwanted truth, the more I resemble my neighbours. One of the reasons Chris Marker is so important to me is that he's the writer of the second life. Others had gone and lived there, but he was the one who lingered long enough to draw the map. And judging by your showing up at Orly, I wasn't alone in admiring his cartography. In Marker's second life, 'the veils and facades of other people' become the author, in movie after movie. He can reveal something of himself only by showing Tarkovsky and Kurosawa at work, or the French students protesting cuts in education, or a cat smiling in a Tokyo alleyway. In order to touch the documentary roots of his own experience, he rewires the connection through someone else's face, or words, though some of his most reliable and memorable ventriloquisms occur as forms of letter writing.

A couple of years after the drug cocktail arrived, I made the movie you saw called *Positiv*. It was part of the afterlife, the time I was never supposed to have. Perhaps that's why I appear in the movie. Oh, I'm still here. I had set every watch, reoriented every compass, staked every bet on the endgame. And watched with my doctors the steady decline of T4 cells. The march toward the end was measurable, quantifiable, reliable almost. I had a year left, maybe less, when the new drugs were approved, and with them a strange new set of disappointments. How could I forgive myself for outliving the contracted moment, particularly when so many others were dying simply because they were born in the wrong country? I had prepared so well and so long for the end, I didn't know how to receive the unwanted gift of more and more. I think the movie is a kind of grieving for the death I didn't have. Though few others might read it that way.

Here are a few lines from the film:

'You think: it's hardest for your friends. When they met you for the first time, there was no way to know that they would have to bury you one day. You all seemed so young, and while they've continued to age at the usual rate, all of a sudden you've grown so very old, so close to the time of your ending. Mostly you would like to apologize for asking so much of them. Because your slide into sickness is slow, monitored by the machines at the hospital, you don't notice at first that you're any different than you ever were, until they come to visit. And while they are gracious and kind and you love them so much, you read the whole cruel truth on their face. You watch yourself dying there. This look hurts you more than all the fevers and sweats and blind panics, because where once there was love, now there is only fear, and this vague, terrible sense that all this could have been avoided if only you'd been a little more careful, that somehow you did this to hurt them, or that they weren't enough so you had to go out and get more, and after you crossed that line you were never the same.' (from *Positiv*)

After I became positive (AKA seroconverted), I learned how to look in a new way. I could see how a body ages and dies in a single instant, the same way a speech glitch or a DNA molecule synthesize generations of inclination. I used to think that light made us visible, but now I was discovering that bodies could light up, that we were made of bands of illumination.

Our dying selves emitted a very particular quality of light that I saw for the first time in the waiting rooms of Vancouver General, where an entire generation of men had turned into the walking dead. We were sad and angry and defeated and undefeated and beautiful and terrifying and each emitted a light that I could see when I could get over the sheer difficulty and mirror-holding prophecy that each of us became for each other. Today it's me with the facial lesions and the cane. Three months ago I was bench-pressing four hundred pounds, now I can hardly get out of bed. And one day, only too soon, it will be you. But out of the chests of these cane wielders and bent-over skeletons there emerged a rare and beautiful light that I was able to find more reliably as the frequency of my visits increased, and I became involved in the local version of ACT UP (AIDS Coalition to Unleash Power).

I started working on a movie that had a single ambition: it would show its viewers how to see this quality of light, with the added benefit of not needing to be sick or dying! I think I've been working on that movie ever since, in the light that is cast when the door is swinging shut, that final burst of radiance, a summary of light before The End.

1.2
Looking

Chase

I remember instances of looking far more frequently than I remember being looked at. Perhaps that's because I started looking long before I transitioned, frantically searching for ways of being that extended beyond my limited point of view. At that time, the most available objects for looking could be found within the walls of the most popular lesbian bar in San Francisco. A haven for bathroom sex and breakup drama, the establishment was a port for trans men in leather jackets, with deepening voices and attitudes bigger than the building.

It's taken me the better part of a decade to unpack my relationship to those men, strangers whom I relied upon and reviled simultaneously. I used to have a packaged explanation for the contradiction: 'It's not personal, I just abhor their willing integration of everything I find to be so deplorable about men: their attitudes, their behaviour around women, their insecurity, their rage...' Pretty good, eh? The logic of the explanation made sense, but the reality was neither that easy nor that well punctuated. Was it that I was afraid? Was it jealousy? What does it feel like to find safety and comfort in a version of normal that places you higher on the food chain than others? (Must be nice.) And who was I to so casually and callously judge and assess?

The first year of transitioning had me looking at no one. To look up would be to acknowledge, and to acknowledge would invite others to assess. I started getting tattooed to give people something else to look at: skin as armour, images as first line of defence.

In self-defence training seminars, instructors tell women to make eye contact with those who pass them walking down the street. Violence happens less often when humans have the opportunity to connect. Either that, or it's easier for you to identify your attacker in retrospect. I look at everyone now, especially those who are managing the responsibility of being looked at. Eyes as armour, recognition as first line of defence.

When I was seventeen, I saw my first eye doctor, who wrote out a scrip for glasses that wasn't filled for decades. I have enjoyed a world that has grown softer and dimmer, strangers invariably appear as angelic strollers, and because they have only outlines my imagination fills in the rest. Do you remember the moment when Robin Williams goes out of focus in *Deconstructing Harry*? He comes home and his daughter shrieks, 'Daddy's out of focus!' His partner urges him to lie down and drink some tea. He tells his newly bewildered family, 'They thought it was the camera ... but it was me!'

Chase

Only yesterday, I was sitting across from someone who looked familiar on a southbound train. They had their headphones in, thumbs fidgeting on the keypad – business was being performed in a way that no one need notice or explain. 'I see you,' I thought to myself as I kept glancing in their direction, knowing that the music wouldn't stop even if the phone got put away.

My relationship to looking has also changed significantly since I started passing. I might know that I am trying to connect – to queerness, to transness, to Otherness – but what does it mean to be read by another as a seemingly straight white man on a subway? Such unwanted gazes are rightfully feared and avoided by many. I'm reminded of the first book I read authored by a trans man, *Becoming a Visible Man* by Jamison Green. I recall him talking about learning to cross the road as way to manage the fear he suddenly inspired when walking behind women on the street. That impulse, that lesson, that necessity, that responsibility, has never left me.

Mike

It's 6:30 a.m. on the subway and I'm heading across town to a housing demo, when I feel my cheek electrons accelerate until they produce a heat strip running across my face. I follow the warmth toward a pair of eyes locked into my skin, and he looks away, but I stay inside the observation trail until he returns the favour. This question occurs to both of us as we jump into the same staredown: which is greater – our shame, or our curiosity? We offer lopsided smiles from the remains of our faces and then he gets up to leave, taking the rest of my life with him. I can't help but wonder: is this really your stop?

I think what you're describing is the difficulty of being looked at, of receiving a look. It's as if, at least sometimes, we were bearing an aggression, as if seeing were another form of war. What I long for is the safety of the cinema, where I can look out from the dark, where my body has been suspended and I can project myself into other bodies, old and young, crackling and bright. Why else would we need, as you describe, a defence, if there weren't something that needed to be guarded from the eyes of others? How clever that you have created a first line of resistance, remapped the skin as picture play. I wonder, at the risk of sounding a thousand years old, if you could say something more about your tattoos, or your relationship with the one who wields the needles?

Chase

It's a popular line of questioning. What does that one mean? What does that say? Do you regret any? Did it hurt? There are many useful strategies to avoid answering. Get so many tats that people can't distinguish between them, wear long sleeves and/or lie. I've tried each.

My tattoo artist, Amanda, lost her first husband at twenty-eight to lung cancer. One day he was fine, six months later he was dead. We talk about him a lot when I'm in sessions, about our hows, and whys, and lackthereofs; she has many tattoos from and about him on her body. Amanda recently finished a big chest piece on a client who was seeking to have his scars covered completely – it was the final step in his attempt to render his surgical transition undetectable in public. She told me that he was nervous and fidgety when he came in. 'I have another client with scars like these,' she said to him warmly. 'You do?' he said, and then exhaled in relief.

People describe the sensation of tattooing much like having a recently extinguished match dragged across your skin. That said, such metaphors neglect various vital atmospheric components of the experience. Is the story behind the image being laid into your skin or is it being excavated? Does the pain make you remember or are you otherwise occupied and trying to forget? Ask anyone with ink and you will hear at least one story about a permanent skin picture that has no meaning.

A few years into a long-term, life-reorienting relationship, I got a large E tattooed on the back of my left arm. 'What does that stand for, bro?' said the man pulling espresso shots behind the bar on Saturday.

'Ex-girlfriend,' I said.

Inside Out

Mike

When I was a kid, hunting through the loot bag of hand-me-downs that were offered as presents, I was forever breaking into my toys to find out how they worked, performing surgical strikes to see how the inside created the outside. Imagine my surprise when I discovered that my private dream was shared by the state. Two months after discovering I was HIV-positive, I took a phone call at eight in the morning. The voice belonged to Martha, a woman employed by the Ministry of Health. We had never met. She asked me for the names of everyone I had been sexually active with. 'Ever?' I asked. 'Yes, that's a good place to start.' She explained that the Ministry was trying to contain the plague, so it was urgent that all of the people I had had sex with be contacted to ensure that none of them was unwittingly carrying the virus. 'If you had the virus, you would want to know, right?' she prompted in her reasonable voice. I had already undertaken the excruciating task of cold-calling former loves and breaking the news to them, and was waiting for the results when Martha rang. So even though I had tried to do 'the right thing,' I was reluctant to share the news. I told her I would call back and never did, though it made me wonder how so much of my insides had wound up in the display room of the Ministry.

Your movies consistently perform this gesture of turning things inside out, laying bare the technologies of family and intimate relationships, for instance. It's as if you've decided to live your private life in public. Do you ever worry you go too far or show too much? Or is showing too much part of the necessary burden you've taken on as a trans projection?

Is it too much – too easy even – to say that I've learned these tricks from you? The difference between us, at least as I see it currently, is that you rely on images to do most of your talking. And I continue to speak. You are the puppeteer, the grand movie master, moving other people's mouths, writing other people's lines so that you are no longer the one talking. Somehow you make private work public but manage to keep your private life private. It is a familiar trick of documentary and strategic emotional disclosure, I think. Does it ever feel lonely?

Someone once asked me if I thought my experiences over the years with anxiety and loneliness were related to my being trans. My youthful inclination was to immediately say no, as I was resistant to any relationship people might propose between transness and sickness or pathology or pain. But recent news of three suicides in our local trans community has inspired me to amend that response, as the correlations between transness and mental health are far more complicated than they seem, even as I continue to assert that 'being trans' is not to blame. I'm not particularly interested in people making conclusions about my mental health for me, nor am I invested in linear narratives that rely on formulas such as *being trans = generally stigmatized* or *unsupported life choice = depression*. There are lots of reasons why my mental health can be affected; the fact that transphobia is anxiety-producing and depressing just happens to be one of the most straightforward.

As a trans person, I often characterize myself as 'having transitioned,' as if to say that the processes of this metamorphosis are long in my past and therefore not included in my present or invited into my future. Operating within this framework has made it easier for me to isolate emotions, experiences and even people into categories of pre-, during and post-transition, and as such affords me the luxury of leaving things behind in search of stories that are better, more accurate and yet unclaimed.

But understanding this storytelling strategy has revealed profound flaws in my transition-related life logic. Living a life that I identify as being post-transition, or that is identified by broader social opinion, means unknowingly characterizing the most intimate and vulnerable parts of my life as being in the past and therefore not with me today. And though I feel like my life is exponentially smoother than it once was, such a summary of me would be inaccurate and insufficient, ultimately ignoring various other realities like shame.

If I were truly 'beyond' trans – as a result of transitioning – I might not still think about my genitals every time I'm in the men's room. If my transition belonged to the past, I might not still internalize other people's mismanagement of my identity as being my fault. And if I really did believe the transition story that I tell others, I might not still worry that the choices I have made to live in this body will render me unlovable to those I need and want most.

My ability to think through my mental health differently shifted while talking with Zoe Whittall, a prominent Toronto writer and close buddy, as she told me about her own experiences with anxiety. Up until that point, anxiety had been my secret, hidden in my youth by booze and bravado and hidden in adulthood by what I can only summarize as a fortunate combination of comic timing and well-refined public-speaking skills. In that moment, I realized that she had part of what I was looking for. She wasn't overly packaged or highly rehearsed, she was quite simply attempting to integrate who she was then with who she is now, all the while knowing that it might not be who she will be in the future.

Trying to process these devastating suicides reminds me that I am not yet good at having these conversations, and that, in part, I rely on my post-trans passing as a way to avoid these vulnerabilities. Every new project I make begins with questions rooted deeply in this perpetually unresolved yet familiar place. I wonder how many of those who claim a 'post-trans' sensibility live as unaffectedly as they seem, or if we can re-open conversations about the relationship between who we were, who we are and who we might be.

Chase

There is a hornet's nest permanently affixed to the inner casing of my chest; a secret contract I've made with masculinity. Left unprovoked, you may never know the nest is there. However, one swat from an uninvited stick and a swarm overwhelms. Thankfully, the hornets are well trained, rarely flying outside the skin.

Hornet's nests are created by a single female, known as the queen. Like most biologically maternalized subjects, the queen is responsible for creating an environment in which larvae can become adults. In late summer, the fertilized eggs in the nest become female, and unfertilized eggs become male. In mid-autumn, males leave the nest to mate and die shortly thereafter.

Metamorphosis, they call it.

Upon arriving home from her first day at a new job in N.Y.C., my then-girlfriend announced that her handsome new boss had decreed, 'You look just like Minka Kelly!' In the time it took me to Google what that person looked like, I felt enraged. 'Men are disgusting,' I thought to myself. Since when is complimenting someone's appearance on the first day a solid managerial strategy? She didn't seem to share my cynicism – giving him the friendly patriarchal benefit of the doubt – and rather was interested in whether or not I agreed.

She does look like Minka Kelly. And I think Minka Kelly is very pretty. Was I mad at him or was I mad at me?

Mike

I think your hornet's nest of a story is telling me some about the way you want to be touched. Perhaps i what you call 'the secret contract I've made wi

I think it reveals that I am trapped between who I am and who I fear I might be. How do you create yourself anew within well-worn social structures? Is it possible to be somehow separate from the constructions and privileges of masculinity I so deeply fear and abhor? What if my anger looks just like their anger? How do I make sense of my relationship to straight white men? Sure, I might not be straight – how passé – but my whiteness and my masculinity are inextricably linked. At breakfast recently with my friend Jen Richards, a powerful, genius trans writer and cultural producer from Chicago, she told me that shutting up and paying closer attention was not a good enough strategy to step into dialogues about my whiteness and my masculinity. Learn more, struggle less.

Hornets buzz loudest when contained – or ignored.

1.5
Serena

Chase

I keep thinking about that first date I had in Tribeca. Did I ever tell you how it ended? I imagine that I didn't, as I'm far better at starting stories than I am at finishing them. I'm also far better at falling in love than I am at falling out of it, but perhaps that is saying the same thing?

Our candlelit conversation revealed that her unavailability was not just circumstantial, but also emotional. That's not a judgment of her, but rather a conflict with the secret story I had created about our meeting. I imagined that sitting across the table from me would dissolve the barriers that kept her intensely present, yet also hesitating. But I was wrong. Someone can be both before you and disappeared, simultaneously.

Leaving the restaurant, I wondered what story, if any, she had created about the potentials of me. I said goodnight to her under the bleeding light of her Manhattan doorstep, then leaned in to the comfort of disappointment's familiarity. Walking off, I smirked, thinking about the hopeful laps I'd taken around the neighbourhood only hours prior. Catching my reflection in a storefront window, I stopped to fidget with the collar of my jacket one last time and disappeared into the downtown subway.

Mike

Separation is the last project couples undertake together. But often there is a series of dress rehearsals for the final cleavage, including a divvying up of feelings. If you can be jealous for the both of us, then I'll look after our anger, just sign here.

Your letter reminds me of falling in love with Serena. She was a storytelling machine armed with the effortless confidence of the ruling class. I had gone to Calgary to escape the body that kept letting me down – in the years after turning positive my immune system undertook its disappearing act with increasing resolve. This was a long while before the cocktail arrived, and I was certain only that I was dying. After I became positive I told nearly no one – in your father's words, I had turned the world around me into California. I quit my job, packed everything I owned into a single bag and hopped on a bus out of town. On weekends I would steal away to the bus station and make a new set of photobooth pics. How dead am I today? While my no-name pals and I had hoped to resist capitalism via DIY communities and volunteerism, living on the cheap in abandoned industrial spaces, creating no-budget cultures and patchwork communities, here was someone who owned her own car and worked the accelerator with high-heeled shoes that weren't purchased at a thrift store. Two forks appeared next to each plate. Two forks? The more certain she was about what she wanted, the less certain I became about who I was.

A year later, lonely and chronically fatigued, I told Serena I was in love with her. I don't think it had ever occured to her, but she was charmed by the idea. I was so nervous that fourteen sentences were running out of my mouth at the same time, until she put on her patrician smile and patted the couch beside her and told me to sit down and take it from the top. If she said yes, then I would stay in the purgatory of my new home; if she said no, I would resume the purgatory of the old city I had never wanted to leave. Either way, I was hopping on another bus the next day for a film shoot I had scheduled across the country. She said yes and off I went, with repeated promises to return, as if we'd been raised on the same fairy tales as children. When I came back a couple of weeks later, she had told everyone she knew that I was positive. Of course, it was the best possible thing that could ever have happened, but it was done without a note of consultation. I was mortified because the California that I was busy recreating had been taken away. Where was my secret country, my forbidden life, the shame that I could water alone, blooming and flourishing in extravagant designs? What she had offered me was the earliest glimmer of a second life, even as I was trudging toward the exit door with my game face on, removing every hint of a footfall, determined to leave no traces. Little did I know.

Chase

Today, I received an email from a very new friend, so new in fact, that calling the relationship 'friendship' is uncomplicatedly premature and entirely one-sided. A few weeks ago we shared a cab en route to a talk she was giving, and we have been getting to know each other since. Though we are newly in conversation, she is not entirely unknown to me because her reputation long precedes her. 'I've been checking you out...' she says to me in an unprompted note. She had found a link to an old movie of mine online, no longer in circulation. My reaction to what might otherwise be interpreted as casual flirtation? Panic.

So I respond, 'Well, if you are going to stalk – please do – allow me to provide you with links to more recent work.' Of course, the delivery was effortless and casual, as if to suggest that I was doing her a favor, and not rapidly attempting to populate her imagination with less vulnerable content.

My work has changed substantially over the past few years, although sometimes I wonder if the shift is actually a subconscious response to the way earlier work was made

How might I package vulnerability and fear in new, more theoretically intricate and exacting ways? How can using the 'first-person' be productive beyond the singularities of one's personal experience? And how can I resist sentimentality – and its related musical genres – in favour of a criticality deemed necessary in public discourse to promote change?

When I started making movies, I didn't know how to edit. However, the moment I encountered the blade tool, I understood the power and necessity of a cut. To stop someone from speaking in order to make room for someone else's thought.

To slow images down, only to implement them again at full speed. To find music as my only narrative reprieve. It was magic. I was cutting films about issues and relationships that were failing, and yet I was making it work. Such sweet, ironic, secret sorrow.

Mike

How can we talk about the things we don't want to talk about? Isn't that a question that of all of your work raises, but perhaps your early work most sharply because there are fewer layers of meta-gloss to distract me from the feelings so openly on display? For me there are also other questions at work – how did Barthes put it when he rewrote the history of photography as a family story, as the story of his mother and himself? He said there was a compelling and irresistible moment in the image, like you he called it a point. He named it the punctum, literally 'the piercing point.' What does it mean to be seen by a picture, and more than seen, to be pierced and wounded by an image?

In the first life it was enough to borrow someone else's idea of the future, but here in the second life it's every woman-turned-into-a-man for themselves. It's not simply that words matter so much, but that you are turning into language at the same time that you are turning into a guy. I am the stories I tell. Little wonder there are so many of us crowded at your bedside.

Chase

I started making movies when I stopped going to parties. When drinking is 'an activity,' all forward movement is stalled in favour of related events.

As a result, my priorities became internal, and the logics of my life started shifting. I called a friend, asked for an editing tutorial, and stayed up late learning. Instead of going out, I stayed in. Instead of hiding beneath bravado, I started visually reorganizing my shame. I'll never forget the magic of that incredibly basic editing, or my reliance upon songs as stand-ins for sentiments that I couldn't make images communicate. Today, those early projects feel like attempts to wrap glass bottles in tissue paper. Pretty, but unprotected. Covered, but perpetually ripping, and forever on display.

Mike

Isn't every movie on display? I think you're suggesting that some movies, perhaps even most movies, are in the business of hiding what they show. Perhaps the way we show ourselves is also the way we keep our secrets. Who are we together, if not the history of our hiding? All of your work, and this writing work between us is no exception, begins as autobiography, the always-shifting story of a life. There seems always more to unpack, to uncover, to get down to the roots of your experience inside the darkness of family.

Chase

When I was little, my mom was hospitalized repeatedly. It was well over a decade before I learned more about her institutional disappearances, and it was summarized to me at that time quite succinctly: when I turned eight she started having flashbacks. Up until that point, the violence in her life, as far as she knew, did not exist. It took me growing, appearing and behaving like the small girl she once was, to trigger the impending avalanche. For me, the lesson implied beyond the obvious was that more than thirty years of not talking about things might actually kill you. That, and maybe: don't have kids.

Mike

When I land in Amsterdam, Jankees is already there with a pouch of salty licorice and a smile so large you could dock ocean liners on it. It's still too early for the city's breakfast establishments, so we are huddled in one of the airport's subterranean getaways, a low-ceilinged cafeteria that looks like an outtake from the Cold War. Jankees and I chat excitedly as I reach into my suitcase for the three bottles containing the chemical elixirs that are keeping me alive. At the next table a man who looks like he died sometime in the last century begins to speak in a stage whisper. He's talking to himself, but the words are so loud that everyone in the room can hear them. It's all in Dutch so I can't pull the grammatical fineries into focus, but he keeps stealing glances at the pharmaceuticals spread across our table and saying something about Jews and death and how the camps should have killed all of us. Jankees is mortified at his country's new self-appointed ambassador and wants to leave right away. Watching my large friend suddenly appear so small, and not fully understanding the language, I gather up the courage that only jet lag makes possible and plant my face well inside the comfort zone of our unwanted companion. 'Do you have something you want to tell me?' I shout, though our noses are nearly touching. He looks like he lives in that forgotten lounge, but now he gets up to leave, still muttering half-syllables to himself. Later I wondered how he was able to read my HIV status from the prescription bottles – no doubt he knew someone who was positive. In fact, he might have been positive himself, though it didn't stop him from spreading his personalized form of plague-speak, playing at once the parts of condemned prisoner and commandant.

Here is Anne Carson on the painter Francis Bacon: 'Bacon says we live through screens. What are these screens? They are part of our normal way of looking at the world, or rather our normal way of seeing the world without looking at it, for Bacon's claim is that a real seer who looked at the world would notice it to be fairly violent – not violent as narrative surface but somehow violently composed underneath the surface, having violence as its essence.' One of the most helpful things she's getting at here is how much looking is not looking. It makes me wonder: how do I see the world without looking at it? And does the violence come from looking toward or looking away?

Chase

I think that looking away is a survival tactic, a strategy of the self that strictly adheres to a desire to see specifically rather than to see generally. It is, after all, impossible to see everything at once.

After more than a decade of estrangement, my dad and I have recently reconnected. A while ago, my sister was scheduled to have lunch with him and encouraged me to join. 'I don't have anything to say to him,' I responded, almost affectless – which of course was quite affected. 'Come on, he's not who you think he is,' she said.

She was right. Once angry and distracted, my dad has softened considerably with age. His indignation has been replaced by regret, his defensiveness supplanted by gratitude and his whisky traded in for wine.

At present, my dad and I are attempting to get to know each other again, to see 'the now' outside the lens of 'the then,' to experience the parts of each other always presumed and never actually spoken. In the time we were estranged, I transitioned and he had a heart attack – facts that, as far as we can tell, are not related. There are so many things we can't see yet, as they are simultaneously too close and too far away for focus. When saying goodbye recently, he extended his hand for a shake in lieu of greater affection. 'Sorry, I don't know why I did that,' he muttered.

Processing the occasion later with my mom, she mentioned that his dad had only ever hugged him once, in a moment of emotional panic right before his death.

Mike

Who would we be without our hugging lessons? I rarely hug my nephew, Jayden, who favours a disaffected slouch, the wonder of his twenty years casually shining off him. As an only child and my parents' only (official) grandson, he is filled with love arrows from every direction, a burden he appears to carry lightly, except for a chronic stomach malfunction that he fuels with bottomless soda lunches. Little wonder that Jayden prefers to remain on the couch when others arrive, offering greetings from a country that is so high wired and anxious it needs to appear as an always-reclining onlooker.

The smoothness broke down only once, not long after his parents had split. I asked him how he was holding up, if he felt some pressure to take sides, for instance. Jayden has a habit of looking up in quick searching probes, absorbing bright screenfuls of information that he furiously processes while looking away, all the while affecting the easygoing postures of his country-and-western icons. But he was looking back at me now with a face twisted up into a knot of painful reminders. There were too many words and not enough time – we hadn't had a conversation like this before and he wanted to short-circuit this one as soon as possible. But he was also stuck, caught between the worlds of how things were supposed to be and how he actually felt. He had been looking after everyone else for so long it was hard for him to know what his own needs might be, so he finally exclaimed in distress, 'What do you want me to say?'

One of the ways I can feel the ordinary violence that Bacon describes is how people make pictures today. While I am the only person in the city without a portable phone, all around me I see newborn photographers and archivists wielding their telephones, madly creating doubles of everything around us. In the old analogue world, you brought the camera body close to your body, swapping your eye for the camera's. Today we push our phones away from us, away from the unwanted feelings of the body we are trying to escape, and the violence of this moment. The camera-phone appears as a kind of shield, held out in front of us, and then the picture appears before we can see it, as if it were already there. After the shutter blinks, there is no further developing required, there is no space after the picture and none before it. Call it digital oblivion or digital eternity. Depending on whether you're an optimist or a pessimist.

As soon as the picture appears it needs to be confirmed, like a citizen of the Catholic church. And no confirmation can be complete without a public reckoning and acknowledgment. As soon as the picture is made, digital scrums muster to confirm that the picture is there, and then it doesn't ever have to be seen again. The digital camera recreates seeing as a way of throwing away experience, even as each picture is archived for potential review 'later on.' The archive means that this moment will be always available, and because we can see it anytime we want, we never have to see it at all. The digital camera has replaced the medieval practice of banishment and makes visible the everyday violence of looking that we can't bear. Where do I send my thank-you notes?

Chase

I was recently in conversation with Riva Lehrer, a painter in Chicago. She's made a career of intricate portraiture and drawings of disabled and otherwise stigmatized bodies. For her, the portrait is a process of power reorganization both for herself and for her subjects. 'The relevance of traditional portraiture is changing,' she said as we mused over her new project, *The Risk Series*, for which I was soon to be sitting. Painted portraits, as a historically colonial project of distinction, were originally commissioned to eternalize the significance of a subject. Further, portraits point to the relationship between the painter and the sitter, as the process of painting was intimate and lengthy. Hours were spent in proximity sitting, talking, holding, waiting and painting. What can we make of these relationships in the present day of immediate image editing, filtering and deletion?

What I read in your musing is that pictures used to be difficult to make, and much more rare and therefore precious, and you feel that slipping away. It makes me wonder if the picture, as you describe it, is no longer the project. Riva's *Risk Series* invites subjects to insert themselves into the picture process. After every session she leaves the studio, and the subject is invited to modify, edit, respond to and/or destroy the work as they wish. The finished product will be called *Chase Joynt by Riva Lehrer and Chase Joynt*, a collaborative method of new image creation, if you will.

Mike

What is the name of that beautiful Joni Mitchell record? *Both Sides Now*. All of your work invites its viewers to look at both sides now, as if we can never have a face unless we have two faces. As our scientists remind us: intelligence is social. Science is not made from lonely geniuses working in the sublime solitary of their lab imaginations, but in groups and constellations. Riva's project feels cut from the same cloth. Seeing is also sharing. A picture, or what we might think of as a 'real likeness,' is made from both sides of the camera. Otherwise it's back to the drawing board.

How do we make a picture? Does this seem like a strange question to ask, when the task has been so simplified that what was once the province of specialists now lies in everyone's hands? Isn't everyone with a portable phone already a photographer, filmmaker, artist? The old saw insists that pictures are captured, but I don't think it really works like that. I think that pictures are made from both sides of the camera, a 'real likeness' arrives when the photographer makes themselves visible. Without this reciprocity of seeing, the act of making pictures is only taking. And the pictures of taking that fill our news reports and movies rarely have power because they have no roots. Making pictures is an art of stereo, it arrives from two sides at the same time. Riva's invitation to remark your own portrait allows this double vision to occur: four hands good, two hands bad.

I remember making a picture of my pal Sofia. Soon after it was made she rang me and announced she was in love with me and then produced a series of increasingly eccentric excuses as to why we couldn't meet up. *You're everything to me, therefore I can never see you again. I'm either or or off with you, don't trouble me with middle-class emotions.* In the picture she is seated at her kitchen table, the light pouring in from an overhead window, casting her in silhouette. In the foreground I'm holding a mirror that reflects moments of window light back up into her face, lifting the darkest of her shadows into something nearly visible. The picture doesn't arrive all at once; instead it requires an approach, and in this instance the approach is made from the side – going head to head felt dangerous somehow, not to mention unnecessary. Instead, the two of us inch together sideways, using our ordinary words to cover up the fact that we are moving closer, until the stereo of the picture arrives via the hand-held mirror, which pours the window light into a soft burnish for her perfect face. She lights up for an instant before a passing cloud allows her to return to a mystery that I will very likely never see again. Perhaps she was trying to coach me in this elementary lesson: sometimes making a picture together is another way of saying goodbye.

Chase

I just got back from Oakland, where I am making a movie about the father of an ex-girlfriend I dated while we lived in L.A. In preparation for our shooting, she brought out a giant collection of photos from her past, and we systematically threw away nine out of every ten pictures of us together. Strangely, this is not the first collaborative ex-expungement of the year. Just last month I got an email from another ex, now a close friend, who made the choice to downsize her baggage. Literally. 'I realized I didn't need to hold them to keep you,' she said.

I have one shoebox full of letters, memories, pictures and trinkets. I call it my ex-box. I haven't looked through it in years. Its existence is an ever-present reminder that an archive is not necessarily a path to holding or remembering.

Mike

The computer is also an archive machine – how convenient for the new security state that Edward Snowden has pulled up the curtain on. Every message and mail, every kissing pic and song selection, all of my preferences have been ordered and arranged. Today, even those who pride themselves on creating messes that can't be cleaned up have been recast into the roles of archivists. It seems we have reorganized our culture around these archive machines, and I can't help wondering why. Perhaps it's because at the heart of our culture there is an anxiety about loss. Why else would we go to such lengths to produce archives of the most trifling concerns?

What is it that we are afraid of losing? Or even: what have we already lost? Are computers the sign that we have lost something precious to us, something we used to have? Perhaps we used to think of this absent piece as part of our home, and now that it's gone missing, we have machines that arrange every last detail, deliver us to every decisive moment except the one that really matters because it's already gone.

Chase

I'm connected to thousands of people I don't know on Facebook. I used to think it was because my work was resonant, but I understand it now as a network-of-knowing to which the specificity of who I am, or what I do, is somewhat irrelevant. Young trans people reach out via the Internet to find safety in the literalized existence of others. We inhabit public worlds to help us make sense of ourselves through the sense-making strategies offered by those around us. Of course the connection is a sometimes knowingly pursued fiction, but nonetheless, I gain insights into the happenings of others via status updates and photos.

Recently, a young trans man in Europe was undergoing phalloplasty. As he reported his progress daily from the hospital, I couldn't help but attach to his posting patterns. The procedure was arduous and extensive; it involved multiple surgeries, extensive recoveries, infections, related complications, tubes, scars and catheters. 'Feeling over the moon!' he reported beneath a picture of a thumbs-up hospital-bed selfie. 'Have an infection! Going in for emergency surgery now!' he posted beside another thumbs-up and a smile. 'Dysphoria is gone!' he finally announced through oxygen tubes and IV lines, along with the disclosure that he cannot walk and will not be able to do so for quite some time. *Dysphoria*, of course, is a word given to him by medical providers as shorthand to describe feelings about his gender, which has been deemed non-normative or incongruent. Watching his journey is crushing.

'Dysphoria is gone!' What does that even mean in this context? Every update is followed by an exclamation point, maybe because he has learned that having surgery is a privilege for some, and therefore he should be grateful or at least perform gratitude in public. He summarizes every infection as a necessary and welcome setback, while the end goal of a life lived on the other side of the binary remains the same, and he is uplifted by a community of people leaving him words of encouragement under his pictures.

But what if we backed away from the selfies for a moment, or even the comment tags, all invariably rendered in close-up? What if we took in the scene from a distance, a telescopic distance even? Would the long shot reveal that the penis is, in fact, not the problem to be solved? What if it was not a requirement of public transition to be satisfied or excited? What if the only reliable narrative reprieve is one where the endpoint continually shifts and changes? Dysphoria, indeed.

Mike

I think you're suggesting that we are all artists showing our work in the new master gallery of the interweb. Our symptoms are an artist's way of cherishing and transforming deeper hurts. Perhaps heaven is not one penis away, though I would like to join your overly medicalized friend in building his picket fence of exclamation marks. Maybe you're also suggesting that the goal of a transitioned body might be concealing another kind of shift that his new surgical mothers and fathers might be less able to assist.

It is Wayne Koestenbaum's assertion that 'bodies have always wanted only one thing, to be aimless.' I have no idea what this astonishing statement means, or how one might lump every body into a single body. Is that the fantasy? But the hope he is expressing, I think, is that a body, some body, any body, but particularly his body, might be aimless. Unaimed. I think he is telling us that his body is aimed all the time. And I think most of us are. Aren't we?

The last time we met, you kindly consented to performing your weekly testosterone injection for my one-minute-per-shot movie project. What could be more aimed than a needle? And without an aim, how could your gender choice maintain itself? How could anyone who has become HIV positive survive without taking the drugs, without taking aim at the illness and the body that hosts it? The simplest acts of shitting, eating and walking, most of these imply an aim, however temporary. But I find the author's hidden request so touching – it is also my hope that I might be relieved of aims and ends and useful hours.

How else to reconcile this old saw about cannibalism that became the key to unlocking the mystery of my own flesh? 'Take, eat, this is my body.' As a child I said yes by eating, by taking experience into my mouth, and I rejected it by spitting it out. Either: *that's me!* Or else: *that's not me!* Everything I accepted became part of my body, even though the old Jesus pics celebrating his tortured and bloodied flesh showed me too clearly the cost of living in a body.

My doctors have worked up pill regimens that keep my viral loads from overtaking my second life, but what they haven't been able to manage is to offer a reason why. Is there a pill for that? Or are we condemned to the talking cure together, telling our stories so that we can unlock the reason to take one more step, spinning our stories like Scheherazade performing for her captor, in the hopes of making a future we are guarding ourselves against at the same time? Today it's not food that enters my mouth, but words, sometimes by unmet comrades like Wayne, but more usually by you. Your words are not keeping me alive, they are my life. When I'm alone, I like to repeat them until they begin to sound like my own. This is the catch-22 of the second life. Every gesture that makes you free also builds the cage. Will we learn to call that love too?

Second Life

'Yes, and this is how you are a citizen: Come on. Let it go. Move on.'

— Claudia Rankine, *CITIZEN: An American Lyric*

They decide to meet each year in the Café of Silence, as they like to call Ten Belles now, the modest bistro parked just outside Marker's last apartment, where they sat only last June without two words to rub together. Mike is tired – some mornings it feels like he was born tired, and he welcomes it, it produces exactly the feeling of homecoming. Each sugar cube in the bowl, each wobbly reflection in the stainless-steel flatware, appears like display items in a golden museum. He is so used to hearing Chase's words inside his head that it is startling to hear them occasionally launched from across the table.

A commotion at the counter, angry words, a cup drops. Heads turn while they savour the perfect French coffee. Mike wants to take his accomplice's hand and lead him to the back of the resto where they can curl up together like cats, home at last. He wants to tell Chase how often he pores over their correspondence, how his letters are more real than dinner, but he's seen in the past how any kind of needful expression can be met with a sudden and irreversible withdrawal.

'It's good to see you, but I can feel my heart running double-time. If I was writing you a letter, the words couldn't hit the page fast enough, but now I'm trying to find...'

'Yes, I know.'

Chase reaches a tattooed limb across the table and steadies Mike's hand, which keeps moving back and forth as if he's trying to erase something.

'I care about you very much, you know? How do we work so you can feel...'

A single shot rings out and a shuffle of exclamations. Chase turns his head and Mike follows the gaze toward the cash where a heavy-set man is emptying the register with a Richard Nixon mask on his face. An errant sunbeam catches the safety on the service revolver and they look away.

'I guess they really hate Americans here.'

Mike starts to laugh but Chase cuts him short; everyone else is already crouched underneath their tables along with their dogs. The sour smell of fear. The inhalation from the head of the room. The collective project of waiting. Footsteps across the tile and then the door swings shut again. A hiss of profanities. They watch Richard Nixon jump onto a scooter and fling his mask off, the sagging plastic jowls hitting the pavement and rolling until the face looks up into a blank and incomprehensible sky, frozen into a smile. As they brush themselves off, they know two things for sure. That they will never come back to this café, and that they'll never write about the event, it's too precious to leave a record. Chase squeezes Mike's hand into his. They don't move for a long time, though the conversation around them rises to delirious levels as if to make up for the silence everyone observed without having to be told. They don't say a word.

Chase

For years, my mom kept asking me to accompany her to see my grandmother. At the time, my grandma was living in an assisted-care facility on the outskirts of the town in which I grew up, a rich, white, *Stepford Wives*-inspired place. I never wanted to be in that town again, let alone its outskirts. I had left home for California at eighteen as a blonde-haired, over-achieving girl with a boyfriend, only to return almost a decade later as a tiny-moustache-sporting, tattooed man. Such a trans-formation rendered details like my prior overachievements and past boyfriends narratively insignificant to the majority of people I encountered thereafter. And other than acknowl-edging awkwardly obvious and unnecessary statements – 'Heeeeeey, you look so different these days!' – I hadn't felt the need to explain anything to anybody.

My grandmother was a wicked woman. It's a strange thing to try to remain sympathetic to someone so cruel. Something about cycles of abuse and realizing that she was acting out on her kids in the ways she was acted out upon. As if her manic hysteria were somehow the only available resource to her, and therefore we, as her kids and grandkids, were supposed to forgive and forget. In the most recent request for my company, my mom told me that Grandma was dying, and while yes, she had ostensibly been dying for decades, the time to visit was really now or never.

We drove out to the nursing home together on a frigid, snow-blown January night. A dutiful daughter, my mom had been making these trips periodically, all the while acknowl-edging that such care for her would have never been reci pro-cated. On the drive, mom warned me that Grandma was uncomfortably thin and not particularly lucid. The Sunday prior to our visit, she got angry about the lunch options, and clogged the toilet with her dentures in revolt. Her teeth had not yet been replaced.

The walls of the home were painted a mute green and smelled of alcohol swabs. Walking down the hall to my grandmother's room, I felt my stomach contract involuntarily. The silent combination of anger and potential shame was only mitigated by what felt to me like game-day adrenaline. If Grandma was going to fuck with us, I was going to be ready.

My mom and I locked eyes knowingly and shared a deep breath as we approached the curtained-off area. But before we could turn the corner, a nurse sporting oversized scrubs and a seventies lesbian haircut stopped us in our tracks.

'I'm so sorry ... but she just passed.'

We froze.

'Right now?' I asked quite genuinely, even though I'm sure it sounded extremely sarcastic.

'Just moments ago,' she said.

As if we were trapped in the second act of a Neil Simon play, my mom's younger brother and his wife surreptitiously emerged from the elevator to join us for the news.

'Right now?' my uncle asked in disbelief.

'Just moments ago,' the nurse repeated.

Outside every room at the nursing home were small glass vitrines filled with trinkets and memorabilia specific to each patient behind each door. Walking the corridors, one might assume that everyone infirm was a war veteran, or in love with one. I gazed upon the gold frames, tiny ceramics and fake flowers staged in the box on my grandmother's behalf. Even if she hadn't been dead, her memories certainly were. My mom reached for her cellphone, and my aunt followed the nurse down the hall.

'Well, Chance, I'm not really sure what to say,' said my uncle.

When I changed my name to Chase, I did not consider its

associative similarity to the word *chance*. Nor did I understand the confusion that would ensue when Chaz Bono decided to transition and choose something so phonetically similar.

Anyway, my mom returned from making calls and excused me from talking to my uncle by requesting that we speak for a moment in private. A generous, soft-spoken woman, my mom's conversion from Christianity to Orthodox Judaism in the year prior continued to intensely inform all of her choices.

'In my faith,' she said to me quietly, 'we never leave a dead body alone.'

'Okay,' I responded quite plainly, as if I had just been given the weather report.

'And I have to go make arrangements for the funeral home to come pick up her body, so I need you to go sit with her.'

Walking through the curtain, I wondered what it must have felt like to call that room home for so many years. Turning the corner to see her, I was immediately overwhelmed. The staff hadn't unplugged her from the ventilator yet, which meant that a machine continued to rhythmically pump her chest up and down. She couldn't have weighed more than eighty pounds. Her lips looked dry and her fingers were purple. I sat down and held her hand.

'Well, now at least we know,' said my aunt as she walked in and sat beside me.

Nobody wants to admit the limits of their labour when taking care of a dying person, but everyone knows that those limits exist.

My uncle followed her into the room with my mom just a few steps behind.

'So, I guess it's probably time we bring out Bill,' he said.

Bill was my grandma's second husband.

'Bill?' asked my mom.

'Grandma has been hiding Grandpa in the closet!' exclaimed my aunt.

Crossing the room where Grandma still lay, my uncle shuffled through boxes of clothing and shoes in the bottom of her closet to reveal a large, bronze-plated urn cast into the shape of a golf bag.

'She wanted to have him close to her, so we hid him under the shoes!' they said proudly.

My mom looked as if she were attempting to contain a mouthful of marbles while sneezing.

The urn was set on the side table now, making us a room of six: aunt, uncle, Mom, me, dead-but-still-breathing Grandma, and dead-but-in-a-golf-bag Grandpa.

'It's a very nice urn,' I said.

'It is,' said my uncle. 'I wonder if we could put her in there too?'

'In the golf bag?' questioned my mom.

'Well, they wanted to be together forever,' said my aunt.

Without so much as skipping a beat, my uncle reached into his pocket and revealed a Swiss Army knife attached to his keys.

'Do not open that urn in here!' yelped my mom.

We laughed. The anxiety in my stomach was momentarily replaced with such excitable glee that I could have opened that urn with my teeth.

The nurse returned to the room with paperwork that she needed everyone to sign. We asked if she could turn off the respirator while she was there, and with a flip of a switch, the room went silent for the first time.

'I'm gonna need some whisky after this,' said my uncle.

We said our goodbyes in the parking lot before the funeral home people arrived to take grandma away. According to the care staff, watching a body leave the building in a bag isn't good for anyone. Driving out of the parking lot, my mom and I were quiet.

'They are going to put Grandma in that golf bag,' she said, 'and I bet she's going to fit.'

Mike

In the second life, we can remake family according to preference, like countries that swap bloodline successions for
democracy. We can vote for our new brothers and sisters and
create a second family, even if we wind up acting out the same
old routines. Your final grandmother visit reminds me of one
of my oldest habits, the way I reserve so much of my intimate
life and affections for those who are no longer around. Mark
became a family member soon after he took his last step.

He would always greet me with a wave that came fromthe
end of his scarf, and a *hiiii* that drawled a vowel so long we
could both land on it. He was a front-line care worker, an
animal-rights activist, and when he partnered up with a trans
activist, he became a tireless supporter of all things trans. His
second or third job was working as a movie editor, and we sat
together through six winters, sieving pictures through the
video co-op's computer, his large capable hands interfacing
with bewildering softwares and diva machines that worked
according to their own schedules. I wasn t able to see then the
way his lightness was also a way of erasing every step, as if he
were walking backward through the snow with a broom, leaving no traces. Now you see me, now you don't.

There's only one other person I know who has Mark's
talent for relentless optimism. It was so consistent that I realized quickly that this was something Mark had worked on,
the way others work at making a perfect cup of coffee or
getting down a blues lick on the guitar. Almost every day I
saw him, Mark would offer some recipe for cheer, which he
applied like a bandage. He did it so well that it gave me a hint
of a darkness that was all his own, a darkness that he
performed with an airy lightness, insistently turning it into

something positive and affirming, ensuring that no one would notice. In your words, he always looked like he was 'doing okay,' especially when he wasn't. So much of his behaviour seemed a kind of cover story, like most of us perhaps.

He was a large man with a crooked beak of a nose and soft brown eyes that were better met when the light was low. They were so admitting they hurt to look at sometimes. The way he held himself shrank his stature, even when he was a hot breath away, showing me, again and again, how to make the impossible work. His touch was so effortlessly light that it seemed like I was practically alone, figuring it all out by myself. It was an old magician's trick he practiced, the fine art of disappearance.

We made a portrait of my friend Tom, and then a collection of shorts that signed off with an extravagantly stuttering Porky Pig announcing, 'Th-th-that's all, folks.' Mark had a thing for these farm animals; like me, he was born in the year Chinese folks mark with a pig. And I couldn't help thinking about the ancient woman rooming over the bun shop who reads foreheads; she warned me that every time the pig year rolled in – one in twelve – it would be time to face the music. To face what couldn't be faced.

The year 2007 belonged to the pig, and despite all reasonable warnings, I came to the cinema one April night with no sense of alarm. My whole life used to happen inside movie theatres, every love and hope and failed dream lived and died there. After settling into the frayed velvet seats, my friend Aleesa leaned close and said she had something to share when the curtain closed. Sure, why not? When the film was over, she told me that Mark had hung himself with a dog leash. He was thirty-five years old.

In the following months I was fortunate to meet with some of his friends and family, and in these encounters he would flicker alive in our mouths and then cruelly disappear. His best friend from public school, had his arm tattooed with Mark's birth and death dates on it. His partner told me that Mark had become a spider, and the next day a coworker said that the balcony plant she'd potted in his honour hosted the largest spider she'd ever seen.

For many years Mark and I were busy gathering our small picture harvests and bringing them back into the computer where they could be endlessly re-edited and keep our own secrets company. Sometimes we succeeded too well. In all those years, how many stories did we refuse one another, or never admit even to ourselves?

There had been no previous attempts, he left no note, there was no obvious reason why. When I met his stunned parents in a nearby parking lot and took them into the service, they were convinced that everyone else in the room knew exactly why he was dead. We wanted to know the reasons why, the progression of events, the narrative clasp that would assure us that his death was meaningful, maybe because that would assure us that our lives weren't a random collision anthology.

As long as I'd known Mark he was always telling me, 'No problem.' One leg kicked up behind him, his arm bent into a backward wave, head raised up in the air. There were no difficulties that belonged to others that he wasn't busy patching, mending, attaching himself to. Which made us wonder how someone who had spent his life in service should have left so little for himself. He was busy feeding feral cat colonies around the city. He organized rallies against animal testing, provided years of research and technical support for a weekly animal-rights radio program, working always with the poor and disadvantaged. He has been a model of kindness for me these many years, a kindness it seems that he was able to extend more easily to others than to himself.

Mark is such an intimate and harrowing portrait of your friend. I hadn't known about the dog leash, as it was a detail absent from your filmic storytelling. In lieu of such details, your movie invited me to sit with grieving survivors as they attempted to identify pieces of an unsolvable human puzzle. Your voice is all over the project, in narration, emotional rhythm and pacing. Somehow we know you are always behind the camera, even while you remain strategically out of frame.

I'm constantly searching for ways to have conversations about lost moments, or with people who are no longer around. Once I thought to ask you about your strategies, but then I noticed a picture of Mark you carry with you. He's wearing a mop of golden hair and a gown of green and gold, smiling for his high school graduation. The picture reminds me that our friends never die, that their ghosts can feel more real than present-day encounters. If the wounds are always present, maybe it's only the description that changes.

How Could You Ever Leave Me?

Mike

One of my mother's favourite activities was planning her funeral. We never mentioned it out loud, but I could tell that the many funerals she attended for her friends were dress rehearsals for her own. Perhaps it was the only way to bear the losses. Why did they put the flowers over there? Open casket or closed? Most important of all was the music. The titles shifted over the years, including a dizzying mix of traditional church hymns, Springsteen anthems and country heartbreakers, but there was one song that featured on every playlist: Leonard Cohen's 'If It Be Your Will.' At last my mother could be the DJ, not to mention the director of her final scene.

My mother is not alone in her funeral reflections. It's an occupational hazard of everyone who has made it as far as their second life. I remember attending a dress rehearsal for my sister's wedding. Why don't they do this for funerals, I couldn't help wondering. It was another sunny April afternoon when I cycled over to Mark's place. He had died a couple of days earlier, and emails sent in the bruised aftermath announced there would be a modest gathering of familiars in the early afternoon, followed by home-brewed death rites that evening. When I pushed through the open door, a man in a wheelchair whom Mark had been looking after told me that his family was coming in a couple of hours and that we had to clear out by then. Yes, of course.

The living room was dominated by a wooden casket that was easily the largest object in the postal code, a painful reminder of just how much of him there had been. No one said a word in there – it was as if he were sleeping inside the box and we didn't want to wake him. Perhaps we didn't want to wake ourselves. I stood quietly breathing in the fresh pine and then walked outside where the wheelchair crew had already started cocktail hour. His partner soon appeared in a breathless rush of Quebecois explications. She was sporting a crisp razor cut, though her skin looked greyish and dull, like it had been left inside the wax paper too long, but as usual she had the energy of ten mere mortals. 'Come inside!' she shout-talked to us and then strode over to the stairwell that divided the living room from the kitchen. 'This is where Mark hung himself!' she announced, and we all took a step back as if we were afraid to get some of the mess on us, and then she proceeded to give us a moment-to-moment recount of the morning she found Mark hanging. She might have talked for twenty or thirty minutes, but nobody moved or even dared venture a breath. HOW COULD YOU EVER LEAVE ME? She said things that she's never said before or since, and when she was done, after she had thrown herself at the ghost of him hanging there, and banged her fists against the wall, and shouted against a god she no longer believed in, she walked downstairs and announced that they were going to be married. Right now.

At this point her attention turned to a Native elder who had materialized, a neighbour I guess, and most of the scrum took this opportunity to leave as quickly as possible. We were terrified, awestruck, sad beyond belief, and now she was moving those who remained into the living room where she began unlocking the casket. I conjured up the most gruesome scenarios possible, trying to brace myself for the shock of seeing him again. Had the hanging left scars, were his sublime features misshapen? But no, she lifted the lid away and there he was again, looking as if he would wake up any moment now, and she kissed him and cried and called him a bastard. They had bought rings, she told us, they were planning on getting married, and she held up a baggie filled with hand-crafted swag. She gave me a pair of beaded earrings. 'I want you to put these on him – when his parents see him that will give them a real shock, eh?' she said, cackling loudly. She would cry one moment and then laugh uproariously the next. Every joke was sacred. The way I touched his face was sacred. The way we watched as the two of them were married by the elder was sacred. Everyone cried. She kissed the bride and then we kissed each other. And then she had to put the lid back on because the family was coming. It was time to go.

Chase

Oren Gozlan says 'the ability to make meaning from absence lies in the willingness to give up identifications, to make sense of one's own desire. It is only in the shadow of death, the place of no meaning or prior knowledge, that such movement can exist, and where desire can survive.' Your story about Mark's funeral is shattering. I don't know how to touch it. How to make sense of the desire to read again something that is so hard to read? To see clearly something so rightfully protected from further seeing? It reminds me that we all want to be good at something – at loving, at losing, at showing up – graciously.

The truth is, I'm not convinced that I'm really that good at anything. Malcolm Gladwell claims that you need at least 10,000 hours of practice to be deemed remarkable at something. And while I've done many things for longer periods than that equation demands, it could never be summarized as doing the exact same thing. It's also not lost on me that the subjects who prove Gladwell's theory are all straight white men with lots of money – notably Bill Gates and the Beatles – what a luxury that kind of practice must be.

To assume a kind of mastery is to identify specific boundaries, and then claim control over the contained expertise. No one is good at everything, but some are skilled at locking off the pathways through which disruption arises, and then persisting. It's why some people love swimming pools but often avoid lakes; it's why some people get married and then claim to feel safe. Maybe 10,000 hours of practice just means that fewer and fewer people are granted access to your vulnerabilities and related mistakes?

My friend Lavonn is one of the smartest people I've ever met, though she undertakes a terrifying ritual with her hair each morning. When she wakes it is picture perfect, a dizzy orbit of red spirals moving in every direction that ideas might travel. Her hair reminds me that the head is made round so that thought can change direction. But after feeding her cat familiars, she retires to the bathroom where she patiently flattens out every groove, turning the whole swarming mass into a single crimson wave. The result is not unattractive, don't get me wrong, but it has the feeling of crowd control. This hair helmet assures me: there are no mistakes here.

In her professional life she is paid some serious coin to teach students about the behaviours of heavy metals. In every word she speaks, she is unsurpassed and electrifying. But in her unprofessional life, she is not allowed to make mistakes. Either she is picture-perfect or else she is a worthless piece of shit. It's difficult for her to 'grant access to her mistakes,' as you put it, because each mistake is a trigger that sends her to the same bottomless bottom. It makes me wonder: who do I like to put at the front of the room? Only the most perfect body, the shiniest intellect, the one who can roll out the smoothest sentences? As Adam Phillips reminds us: we use our ideals to punish ourselves.

After Mark died I couldn't let anyone touch me. His death troubled every place I used to call home, because if the cheerily reliable fix-it man could take his own life, then everything was up for grabs. I put myself in a cage and maintained a relentless surveillance using whatever tools I had, which mostly meant overworking on my movies, but when this wasn't enough I reached for Zen. I found a brilliant teacher and he was the one I put at the front of the room. He filled the drop-in assembly with ironic postmodern joy and a hallucinatory form of speechmaking. He was a splendid physical specimen steeped in texts that were thousands of years old, yet in his bold translations they appeared more urgent than the daily headlines. He was also self-hating, blind to anyone's opinion but his own, and a monomaniacal patriarch. The Zen form, at least the way this man projected it, was a perfect way for me to stay locked up inside my problems. I could be in a room full of others believing in the cover story of community; only he was the one doing all the talking.

I think I was afraid to put mistakes at the front of the room. Did I say *was*? I wanted someone who could lay down smooth sentences alongside their stellar yoga practice. But if I could admit someone to the front of the room who made mistakes that could be recognized and acknowledged, this might show me that errors don't need to be fatal. Can we survive our mistakes? Will you still love me when I'm broken and dishonest and distracted? I know what perfect looks like – it's shining back at me from every magazine cover on the stand. Not to mention your newly perfect face. But could we make a life together, could we build a sentence together here in our second life that stammers and fails even as we kiss our way past the inevitable disappointments? As you and I slowly wade our way through the murky grammars together, I can feel us beginning to hold up a newly cherished ideal, the grail of the imperfect.

Chase

Stereotypes flourish about the trans-masculine community. Here is the commonplace: those who start taking testosterone often lose their ability to cry, become rage-filled and behave like teens going through puberty. Visual documentation of this process – made by those transitioning and by others – has emerged as the most frequent format of response to this fallacy of pre-dictated gender behaviour. These videos are most often progress narratives that move from points of previous fracture toward present clarity. I am reminded of Judith Butler's theories of gender performativity, and the social machinery that takes up these claims as proof and trappings of identity. Can I not be a stereotype even if a stereotype might be true? Change and exception are real and necessary political possibilities.

I've cried only a handful of times since having a hysterectomy, which is certainly not the number of times I've had a reason to, never mind the times I've actually been in pain. I suppose I've had to learn how to cry differently since having the operation. I'm not compelled to make a movie about it, though – at least not directly. Instead, I'm motivated to start somewhere in the middle, between the stereotype and the reclamation, between the floodgate watershed and the tears my eyes so often fail to create.

Mike

I never get an erection in a Chris Marker movie. This bothered me as the years went by because he was always my fave director, and there seemed to be something missing. Was this only head-and-shoulders cinema (leaving the knees, the orbits of the waist, the closed eye of the anus, for others)?

Some directors have made me cry, lesser gods in the heaven of cinema, hacks even. When I was undertaking the brutalizing cure for hepatitis, I would be washing the dishes or looking out the window when a flood of tears would begin. It might last five minutes or five days – the new drugs I was taking poached serotonin from my cranial circuits so my crying bouts arrived like weather patterns, entirely unmotivated by events. One afternoon, in a heavily medicated state, even the execrable sequel to the sequel of *The Godfather* brought tears. Of course, it happened during a much-remarked-upon love scene between Al Pacino and an orange. The killing floor was already full, the opera lovers had gone home and the church was empty – all that was left was a final sobbing fit over lost fruit.

I didn't really have a good cry in a Marker film until *Sans Soleil*. The first tear fell after the camera follows a poacher's rifle on the African savannah, felling its giraffe target in a pair of shots that pierce the neck. 'I will have spent my life trying to understand the function of remembering, which is not the opposite of forgetting, but rather its lining. We do not remember. We rewrite memory much as history is rewritten. How can one remember thirst?' Several years later my best friend spilled this all out, word for word, in a doughnut shop we liked to meet in, and I cried to hear her tell it, and then she looked up and smiled. She was quoting and I hadn't noticed. Quoting Marker.

The movie is constructed as a series of letters, but of course you know that already. The cover story for the director's wandering montage is a woman's voice that keeps repeating, 'He wrote me...' followed by the most beautiful sentences Marker ever wrote.

Later in the movie the camera trembles as it meets the face of a woman in the marketplace in Guinea-Bissau. As soon as the camera finds her, everything else feels dull and insubstantial, ghost words in a ghost film. Can a camera long for a face or fall in love? Marker keeps trying to move on, to change his identity, his way of speaking, but always he returns to this moment, this face. What he is showing us, I think, is the wound of being looked at, or the way this face wounded him. After this movie the elusive filmmaker would be wise, funny, off-handed, politically committed, but never again unguarded, never so raw or tender, not even when he shared with viewers his special place in the second life. 'Even if I was expecting no letter I stopped at the general delivery window, for one must honour the spirits of torn-up letters, and at the airmail counter to salute the spirits of unmailed letters.'

Chase

When I was little, I only cried about the important things, like not being allowed to play hockey in the basement, being forced to wear a dress to a funeral and the time I peed my pants because Josh's mom got really mad at me. As a teen, tears were replaced by anger; that is, until I experienced my first heartbreak, and had to do some major emotional reorganizing. Even though I was the one responsible for that breakup, the loss of such seminal adoration has left me indefinitely questioning.

My mom, too, is still mourning the loss of that love. Sam was perfect 'husband material' in her opinion. Granted, he's someone's husband now, so I suppose that proves her point. First loves are responsible for teaching you that love is not enough, all the while instilling the hope that it might be. I remember the potentials of those past opportunities - what would life have been like had I not left him?

One night, while wandering the streets of a sun-setting Paris, Mia and I stumbled upon a dance floor on the bank of a river. Couples of all persuasions waltzed and tangoed as bystanders sipped beer and looked on lovingly. The platform was surrounded by grassy hills that were peppered with revelers and we stood together amidst the crowd, awestruck at the scene. I kept taking pictures, hoping to capture the magic that caused my chest to keep contracting, but everything was blurry, rightfully resisting my desire to hold and keep.

We walked together that evening, all the while knowing that in seven days we'd be separating indefinitely. It's a new kind of love that can admit the failures of affective attachment, and to grant each other patience as we set one another free. She too was documenting the dancing. Later we compared our collections and happened upon a serendipitous moment when I took a picture of her, just as she caught the reverse shot of me. It's the closest I've come to crying these days, these solitary skin sensations, with the tissue of my muscles fluttering rapidly beneath.

2.6
Pride

Everyone in the men's room must think I'm homophobic. Mostly because I was late to learn the codes and lack the requisite decade of boyhood training necessary to smooth the edges of my urinal-proximate behaviour. But also because my strategy for public peeing combines a lack of eye contact with occasionally gruff behaviour – anything necessary to ensure that the person pissing next to me can't see what's in my pants. It's a cruel trick, this perpetually suspended phallus stage of mine, or what did Jung call it? The Electra complex: boys fearing castration and girls having penis envy. Of course, the castration and the envy both remain ironic and relevant in these contexts. Jung determined this phase would resolve at age six, and I'm thirty-three.

My first encounter with gay cruising was in the context of a queer theory class. Having never ventured into men's rooms prior, the realities of these masculine rituals were practical, exciting fictions. These days, when I do look up in the men's room, it is very easy to determine who is, and who is not, looking. More codes to feign ignorance about.

In a recent conversation with my friend Tim he announced, 'I just don't care anymore,' as we processed the realities of long lines, no toilet paper, broken stall doors and peeing while trans in a bathroom. While changing at the gym a few weeks ago, he noticed a man cruising and decided to drop his towel, revealing what he thought might be the deal breaker for the occasion. They left the showers together soon thereafter.

Mike

How did Mark Twain put it? 'Clothes make the man. Naked people have little or no influence on society.' But Twain wrote before the advent of World Pride, where I watched a visiting pre-teen squealing into her mother's face: 'I saw boobies! Boobies!' The game face of adolescent delight is standing less than a metre away from the boobies – they must be magnificent indeed because they have erased any sense that above them lie ears that might hear. Perhaps she imagines that she and her mother are walking in a force field where they cannot be seen or heard, as untouchable as a tourist or a virus, the old suburban dream fully realized at last.

'This is my hangover tank,' reads the dark slip of a shirt that barely contains the hundreds of workouts my sidewalk companion has used to transform his chest into an alien mass of picture-ready deltoids. On his arm a pair of boy accessories keep step, necessary accoutrements for an afternoon like this one. It's World Pride Day in Toronto, after all, meaning 100,000 revellers are stuffing the downtown core with the kind of good cheer that only comes with a heaping dose of public voyeurism.

The invitation is: come naked. Come in the costume of your own flesh. Bring us your potbellies, your love handles, your sagging man breasts. Bring us your flat feet and flabby thighs. The parade floats an endless succession of handsome come-ons rolling past, the rows of muscled abs honed to a sublime shine in anticipation of their spotlit moment. But the parade does not belong to its display models. This is the secret genius of Pride – it must be why so many have come out to play this afternoon. We are the real parade. The sidelines, the spectators, that's where the real action is at.

When I turn down Maitland to begin a serious wade into the assembly, I am quickly overtaken by a posse of leather-bound bottoms, with one or two tops holding their obligatory lariats. For a moment the crush makes us inseparable, and we inch along skin on skin. I smile at a homely boy who looks lost and excited in equal measure. When he pushes ahead of me, I can see the fresh marks he is wearing on his back, signs of his innocence. I can feel in the instant when our eyes meet how much he has left behind. He couldn't speak if he wanted to because of the ball gag, but I don't have to hear the words out loud. *I am beautiful because I have embraced my unwanted shit. I have rung the keynote of every modern alchemy and turned my obstacles into pleasure.*

As I slow my approach to let them join the throng ahead, I wonder what happened to my shame, my beautiful smallness, my cherished uglies hiding in the closet. And why speak about the closet as if there were only one? All of my closets have closets, my personality is only a Russian doll of closets. It's so difficult to touch the bad feelings that inevitably arise when I move toward what I want when I'm out here, amongst the faux-hawks and the whip-meisters and the swimsuit gym adverts handing out flyers for the master's uptown show. Is this the one day on the calendar when the whole world turns upside down and everyone might become, if only for a moment, what they secretly desire? Is that what is being celebrated here?

We are performing our endless display on a hot July afternoon. The parade of our imperfections, the necessary deviations from our televisual role models – the sheer ordinariness is what makes us so special. Why not come right out and admit it? Our flaws and failures make us sexy. I can't help smiling through my uneasiness. I've come here, as usual, as part of a film project. Others require GPS, I only have to point to the compass of my movies. But because I am reluctant to go, I arrive late; 100,000 guests have come before me, and I have no idea where to look. My camera throbs inside its over-heated housing, while all around me people raise their phones into the air as if in salute. I decide to head home and stumble into a modest Falun Gong protest featuring four women meditating on a parking ramp while another hands out pamphlets. Amidst the delirious bass-heavy stomp of the day I come away with a single picture of a woman protesting in stillness, her eyes closed so that she can imagine a place where the state cannot punish her for her beliefs.

Chase

My first Pride was in Los Angeles. I marched alongside my first girlfriend, though we were closeted, and therefore attending under the guise of being allies and friends. Someone in our group suggested we dress up for the festivities, and so it was agreed upon that everyone would represent a colour of the rainbow. If we walked together, we'd make some overly didactic, embarrassing, Pride-worthy scene; but if we walked alone, we'd simply appear hung up on a colour. Luckily, I already owned a pair of orange pants.

I don't remember anything else about that Pride, except that I took my girlfriend home a few months later to meet my family and friends. She later admitted to having an affair with one of my soccer-playing, dude-buddies she met while we were there.

That was the end of the closet for me.

There is no Pride quite like the party thrown in San Francisco. On Castro and 18th Street, a monthly event called 'Brownies for my Bitches' used to boast $2 watermelon shots, snacks, and more lesbians in one place than I had ever seen.

Around 10 p.m., the windows would start sweating.

Of the seventy-five to one hundred people attending these events each Tuesday, I was lucky enough to get to know three. 'I'm going to make out with a girl tonight,' said a stranger with a boyfriend, as she sat at the bar with her best friend. Thirty minutes and two shots later would reveal that girl to be me.

At Pride, you can always tell who has had top surgery the year prior based on the public display of newly constructed chests. Years spent binding with double-layer compression vests is enough to make anyone take off their shirt indefinitely. The parade of raw lateral scarring is always complimented by bands of newly purchased underwear, peeking from the waist-lines of Pride shorts and jeans. 'Look at me!' scream bodies that have so often gone to great lengths not to be seen. 'But let me signal to things you can't see as well, just to keep things interesting.'

Mike

There was a moment in my life when everyone around me knew I was positive. Or so I imagined. A few weeks ago I was driving in a car (a most unusual occurrence) when a closely distant friend asked what my new movie was about. I said it was about AIDS and the years when so many of us were positive without the consolation of medication. A new kind of silence breezed through the car. I realized – but only after the words had slipped out – that no one there knew I'm positive. It was as if I had announced leprosy, and I felt bad for making them feel bad. Or perhaps they didn't feel bad, only uncertain. What does it mean for this person sitting inches away from me to share such a thing? He's not going to die in my car, is he? The words didn't feel like they had any gravity attached until I caught the reaction shot.

The fact that I'm HIV-positive is something that used to be widely known, even assumed. I was making movies about it, but more importantly, it was in the news, it was part of the scenery, some aspect of the landscape we all lived in. And then I remembered again that coming-out narratives don't rush by in an instant. Sometimes it can feel like a full-time job. Though it's only in my second life that I've come to recognize that these sharing instants are not podium declarations, but part of a necessary call and response – it's not only the speaker that is coming out, but the listeners as well. In this moment of opening we take up a political project of re-education together, re-imagining other people as vehicles of happiness instead of threats. Or at least, that's the hope.

One of the binding agents that attaches queer theory to our second life is that, as Lauren Berlant points out, 'social policy should rely on relations of care rather than institutional relations, like of marriage and family, to help to distribute resources for the flourishing of life.' I think she means: sisters are doin' it for themselves. Or: the revolution arrives one conversation at a time. Your coming out helps me to create better fantasies, to stop thinking of my desire as something to be feared. Saying *I love you* always means *I'm ready to change.* The second life is unthinkable without its border-crossing stories; the only way to leave your own funeral is to invent a story you can believe in, and that others can believe in alongside you. So many of us in our first life were stuck because we couldn't dream ourselves into any of the stories we were expected to become, but today many of us are conjuring better fantasies that are not trying to ride up over the awkwardness and bad feelings. We're trying to make room for that as well.

Chase

On most Sunday mornings, my mom drives downtown from her pristine North Toronto dwelling to pick me up for coffee. I spent the better part of a decade in California, so my return to Toronto has ignited a motherly mandate to make up for lost time. Last week, we decided to spice up the routine by wandering off the main drag in search of a park bench. 'I just feel stuck in the middle,' she says as we finally settle, referring in part to this hybrid life she leads, half lived Orthodox, half lived with her daughter and transgender son.

My mom converted to Orthodoxy later in life, which means that she has non-Jewish children, and a host of life experiences that sit outside the confines of Judaic tradition. In 2016 she wears a wig, doesn't touch men that she isn't related to and keeps kosher. In the nineties she celebrated Christmas, swam in swimming pools, and made a mean, multi-ingredient cheesecake. Nobody in her Jewish life knows that I am trans.

My return from California was timed for the eve of her second marriage and the first public display of her conversion.

It was an Orthodox affair, which meant the entire ceremony was divided by gender: men's dancing room, women's dancing room, men's drinking ceremony, women's social hour. It was the first time since transitioning that I was seen with her in public.

Of course, there were a few people in the room who did know our history: my sister, an uncle and a few cousins. Josh, my long-lost childhood friend, was also in attendance. He too is now Orthodox and married with multiple children. Surprisingly, seeing Josh still made sense, as we had always been brothers, though he fumbled awkwardly as he attempted to explain that to his wife.

At the ceremony, my mom asked if I might say a few words on behalf of my sister and me before the dinner reception. I obliged, as it wasn't so much a question as a statement. After the speech, more than a dozen people came up to compliment her on my speaking. 'What an incredibly charming and articulate son you have! How old is he, fifteen?'

I was twenty-seven at the time. My weekly testosterone injections had caused my voice to sound youthfully squeaky.

2.8
Leaving Home

Mike

My doctor's face is a hearth; as soon as she opens the waiting room door and calls my name, I have an address again. Though this is another home I am reluctant to admit. No matter how deep the system failure, I don't manage a visit more than once a year. But only last week, feeling the accumulation of guilt over my missing cell count numbers, I cycled east and climbed the stairs. Chelsea! She is Dr. Chelsea to most, and maintains one of the most steadfast all-HIV practices in the city. A couple of decades back, a doc pal rang up the faraway reserve she was working at and asked her to move into the city and take on some of his practice. Both he and his doctor partner were HIV-positive, though he was still able to get to work. This was back in the days before medication was available. While the city was filled with doctors, few had the stomach to take on a cohort that would die terrible lingering deaths, or sudden violent deaths, our bodies filled with illnesses that hadn't been seen in a century. Within a year of her relocation, her doc friend died, and then his partner died, leaving her with a needful patient overload. It is hard to reimagine this moment – how do you go to work every day faced with a horizon of terminal illness? Chelsea is one of my heroes, endlessly concerned and diligent and laughing all the way. Of course she continues to overwork and two years ago she had a stroke in her office. As a result, she's cut back her hours a bit. Like all of us, she is trying to find a way to take the next step.

In between form fillings she describes a young man who had recently become positive and travelled to see her. The strangest factoid was his address: he called Sudbury home. I couldn't help asking, 'Why does he come and see you if he lives in Sudbury? It's four and a half hours away on a featureless mega-highway.' Chelsea replied, 'Because he can't take the risk of being seen in a doctor's office. He doesn't know anyone who is positive, there's no community, and he's completely in the closet.' As soon as she said the words I realized what a privileged bubble of a community I live in. I can be an 'out' positive person without having to negotiate the labyrinth of societal disapprovals that this young man will have to manage. In other words, my being positive doesn't ask the people around me to leave home. Or so I imagine. One of the reasons for activist art and demos is to stretch the meaning of home, isn't it? Could the stranger sitting next to you on the subway, the one whose face is covered with sarcosi lesions, also be home?

Chase

The year after my sister was born, my parents bought a small, yellow-brick bungalow on the same street as the local hospital. Soon thereafter, a large sign was hammered into the front lawn proudly showcasing a picture of the renovation. My sister and I were enrolled in private schools, and we ate dinner with other families who also lived in enormous houses. Neither of my parents came from money; my mom ran away from home at sixteen, and my dad worked his way up from apprentice sales to corporate business in his twenties. For them, the new house was a physical representation of emotional, familial and financial overcoming.

I loved that house. Just beyond the driveway, a giant oak tree towered over the backyard. In the winter, its trunk became the perfect snowball target and my most inimitable friend. It was in that house that I was gifted a karaoke machine, with the accompanying cassette tapes of *A Hard Day's Night* by the Beatles and a compilation of hits by Whitney Houston. With the basement as my new stage, I needn't worry about the happenings upstairs.

Within five years of the renovation, my mom announced that they were selling the house, and in the months that followed my dad disappeared from our family. Home, in the form of walls and trees and dreams, would never appear in such a form again.

It wasn't until I started falling in love with people that I realized 'to make a home' was a practice and sentiment worth cultivating. To make the perfect salad dressing, to write notes by hand and to wait at the arrivals gate for someone who otherwise assumes they are taking a cab.

Home is now a never-ending quest of my making. Yesterday, I passed a trans woman stocking shelves in the aisle of the local drug store. We locked eyes. 'Home might be here,' I thought.

Mike

If art-making is a 'never-ending quest,' as you wrote me, perhaps part of the hope in setting off on the journey is that it never finds home. It makes me wonder if building movies is another way of leaving home, again and again. Starting a new project may be a form of saying goodbye, setting off for another journey without end. Never mind Google's desire to map every geographical moment (our colonizers have returned as computer geeks) – never arriving means always being a little bit lost. Doesn't it?

Can you be a little bit lost, or is it an either/or proposition? You can't die a little bit, you can't be a little bit of a son. But after Mark died, I started showing up at his townhouse as if we had both lost our homes, and I began making a movie where I was more than occasionally lost. I was trying to resist the impulse to turn his life into a story, to lay bare the selected factoids that could resolve my mysterious friend into a sound bite. I wanted to maintain a necessary portion of his invisibility, his secrets, by making him visible. This is a business-as-usual strategy for higher-ups at security agencies the world over, of course. Hiding things in plain sight. Not incidentally, in the two years it took to make the film following his death, nearly all of his nearest and dearest had moved, as if the fiction of home could no longer be applied.

Chase

On Saturday, while walking back from a DIY film festival held on the outskirts of a streetlamp-less city, our group ventured through a hole in a fence because someone proposed it might be a good shortcut home. Emerging from the brush, we encountered towering piles of concrete, sand-covered garbage and giant tire-tread marks, long locked into place by the relentless summer sun.

'If we just keep walking this way...' one person said, pointing to a group of cars behind a fence in the distance. 'What if we follow that guy?' said another, gesturing to a lone man walking a dog while kicking a broken bottle. We walked through, up and over. It was a scene from one of those nineties movies that inspire nostalgia for childhoods no one really experienced or frankly believes exist.

People start do-it-yourself festivals as a platform for voices, people and ideas that are excluded elsewhere. They might not succeed, but most self-propelled projects tend to align, however broadly, in their resolve to not wait for others to do it for them.

I keep making work, I think, as a way to rip new holes in fences. In contrast to formalizing gates, which would dictate the manner in which people should be entering and exiting the park. I think holes afford opportunities for accessing previously unimagined places. The first hole I encountered was in 2001. I was sitting in a large lecture hall at UCLA awaiting a guest speaker in our Queer Performance class. I hadn't thought to inquire as to who was coming that day, in part because my work at that time was managing encroaching anxiety about my own queerness, and not necessarily in performing as a dutiful, syllabus-stalking student.

The guest speaker turned out to be Kate Bornstein. In a self-reflexively direct attempt to demystify various assumptions people were making about her gender, Kate began her class address by dropping the register of her voice, and then inquiring as to whether or not that 'did' anything to help us figure her out.

'Yes it did!' I thought to myself, silently reeling from the recognition that this was the first trans person I had ever knowingly encountered in public. I know now that such a rhetorical question was posed to highlight the various transphobic expectations we put on trans people in public to be 'educators', but I didn't know that then. 'The thesis of my latest book,' she said, 'is do anything you need to do in order to find a home and to stay alive. Just don't be mean.'

'I can do that,' I said to myself. 'I think.'

Mike

My friend Pat was diagnosed with breast cancer two weeks ago. *Cancer*. Whenever I say the word I try to whisper, and still it sounds like giants having an argument. CANCER. She has three lumps in her left breast that are working day and night to claim as much territory as they can, so sooner than later she will have to leave this wayward breast on the operating table. Sometimes you have a conversation that is also a conversion – you step out of it into a new world. A world in which you no longer have a breast, or at least, you are facing the prospect. Say hello to your second life. And because illness is a deviancy, a wrong that needs to be righted, no sooner is the prospect of loss conjured then its replacement is summoned. Lose a breast, gain a prosthesis. How about a prosthetic attitude? Or a prosthetic morality?

The cancer industry doesn't dazzle Pat with the three-breast Monte straight up; that has to wait until my friend meets up with the city's premiere cancer specialist, a woman Pat refers to as the dragon lady. The dragon lady likes to lean in close and dish openings like, 'Speaking as a woman...' Meaning: speaking as The Woman, the undemocratically elected representative of all woman everywhere. 'Speaking as a woman, I would feel incomplete without a breast. Breast replacement surgery has undergone significant advances...' and then the stump speech begins, the one she's delivered too many times now. Remember: it's not your illness and it's not your breast. I need you to appear healthy because seeing sick people throws a shadow across my morning. Getting a new breast will make you look normal, it will allow you to pass, as if you were someone who had never left parts of your body in the operating theatre. So let's get this straight. You're not doing it for yourself, you're doing it for me, and for all of us in the country of the able-bodied. Only this isn't how the dragon lady puts it. She says, 'I'm speaking to you *as a woman...*' In other words, if you want to be a woman, you'll do what I say. You are losing not only the breast, but your gender, and I am here to restore both.

Two days after her conversation, Pat travels across town to her office where she works as a psychotherapist. Here she is in her own words: 'I'm on the subway and I see a woman in her fifties. She's wearing brightly coloured, stretchy tight pants, sandals and a wine-faded Indian cotton shirt. She has short hair and a lovely face. I like what she is wearing. Then I notice that she has only a left breast. She is an Amazon. So I walk up to her and look her in the eyes and say, "Excuse me. I'm having a mastectomy and I notice you didn't have reconstruction. How is it?" "Great," she assures me. She just couldn't go through another surgery. Recently she was lounging on a beach in her bathing suit when another stranger asked her about it. "That's good," she told me. I think she meant that it was good that people could ask and that she was willing to talk about it. She says her husband liked her breasts more than he liked her. She gives me her card and we get off the subway.'

Even a few days earlier, this stranger would have passed without a hint of notice, but today she's the most important person on the train. The diagnosis is also an initiation rite, an entry portal to a society so secret that its members can live alongside people we see every day, only they're coded so that only insiders notice.

Chase

I was recently invited to participate in a public talk about trans-related research when the subject of my work came up. *Resisterectomy* was installed on campus at the time, and the content overlapped, which made the invitation quite pointed.

Resisterectomy is a moving-image gallery installation that I made in collaboration with Dr. M. K. Bryson, which thinks through the impact of medical technologies on non-normatively gendered bodies, namely M. K.'s double mastectomy during cancer treatment and my hysterectomy during transition. A student mentioned sitting in the room with the work, in part to watch how people reacted to it, and in part just to *be there*.

When questioned about the reactions the student witnessed at the gallery, he responded quite casually. 'People looked at it with disgust.' Another added, 'Yeah, I had a similar experience at the show ... people asked me to clarify for them whether or not it was a man or a woman, a boy or a girl. They tried to get me to explain to them what was going on.' I let the room have an awkward, pregnant beat before responding, 'So tell us! Did you clarify it for them?'

The room laughed. I laughed. And of course my question was left unanswered.

I often think about the consequences of these words, and the purported fussiness of art-work-in-public as teaching. What should I care more or less about – the fact that work is happening in public, the fact that there are trans bodies in spaces where there were none prior, the fact that people can say whatever they want and feel protected from the consequences, or perhaps the fact that as part of my practice I might be contributing to the wrong assumption that teachers and makers should provide a protection service that offers moral-free reaction shots?

Mike

Wait, wait. Disgust? People were taking in your show while around them swirled registers of disgust? I know what this means but I don't know what this means. The heaviness of that word. Where do you carry it, how do you hold that, the disgust of strangers directed toward you? I've no idea how you manage with those swearing allegiances to their fear, but your recounting makes clear how you massage the afterglow in the classroom. As soon as they raise the spectre of prejudice and hatred, you crack a joke that isn't a joke. 'Well, did you clarify it all for them?'

Last night I watched again the little shot we made in your warehouse getaway. I'm recording sound and picture separately, so I ask you to clap; on traditional movie sets there would be a plastic clapper with the name of the director and the movie on it, not to mention someone assigned to the task. But how could you know this? I ask you to clap, so you start clapping, like a good audience member following their cue. After a few rounds you look over at me and smile, and I can't help thinking: you smile like a girl. I don't mean that smiling makes you look girly, but that girl-women have this thing they do to make things okay for others. The more gritty and uncomfortable, the bigger the grin. *I am feeling so awkward right now, but what's most important is that you feel okay. Let me smile away your difficulties.* I have seen you flash this smile, yes, this very same smile, so many times already. I've seen you reach for it as a kind of reflex even. And it strikes me, as I play back your smile parade (which is warming and filled with promise and makes me want to jump into your arms), that this smile is also a way to remove yourself from the scene. *Oh sure, I'm going to make things okay for you, but there's a cost, no doubt about it. Because after this smile I'm leaving my body behind and going to that faraway place that is so secret I can't even name it myself. There is a world without maps and borders, without road signs or alphabets. The place before feelings start, before sensations are converted into opinions. Catch me if you can.*

Perhaps your smile is part of a masquerade, a binary-breaking, post he said–she said gender drag. To quote Paul B. Preciado, author of *Testo Junkie*: 'For the Zapatistas, given names and balaclavas work in the same way that the wig, the second name, moustaches and heels work in trans culture: as intentional and hyperbolic signs of a political-sexual transvestism as well as queer-indigenous weapons that allow us to confront neoliberal aesthetics. And this is not through a notion of true sex or an authentic name, rather through the construction of a living fiction that resists the norm.' Your smile, and the joke you smooth out the classroom with: is this the living fiction that resists the norm?

Chase

I think about this often, about strategies of engagement, and the available tools of this trade. I'm aware that my smiles and my ability to joke are made possible on account of how I look and sound. I am white, masculine, passing and highly attuned to the specific social cues that allow me to code-switch so successfully. The roots of code-switching stem from linguistics, and are prominently historicized in black communities where people shift their speaking between more formal and less formal styles. For me, the *living fiction* is tied into this kind of formal styling: what do I need to sound like in order for this room to hear me? How can I – whenever I'm given a chance – help reshape the space between what people are looking at and what people actually see?

Mike

I think I hear you saying that before we talk, a conversation has already taken place. Inside the green room of the public self, gestures are required so that you can be heard. And the implication, I think, is that if you didn't do the necessary prep, you might be misheard or silenced. For instance: you might be named disgusting. Again. Because you wear the marks of your second life on your body, in your clothing choices or tat camouflage, you keep reminding me that gender is a construction zone, and that I keep listening to the same tall tales in order to stay on one side of what used to look like a tale of two cities. Helping people to wake up to what they haven't noticed is a bit like being elected mayor of a city no one wants to live in. Who wants to take on the extra stress and strain?

2.10
Duty and Profit

I always think about sex as it relates to some of your questions. Like: why do all those self-help blogs about dying have every dying person confessing that they wished they had been more 'free' and had 'more sex?' What would that free sex look like? And does that sex fit into the rest of the life they wanted and lived, or was it a different life entirely? And then what? Where is *that* blog?

I am lucky to have a body that works, mostly in accordance with my needs. Having survived surgeries, injuries and histories of violence that could have destroyed various capacities, I remain remarkably intact. That said, sex remains the penultimate brain game.

'It's like shooting fish in a barrel,' says my friend Tim about the potentials of finding sex online. 'Just don't overthink it.' Up until that point, it hadn't occurred to me to pursue sex in this manner, because I don't trust most men. The first ad I posted was somewhat formulaic and avoided any detail that might disrupt my desired anonymity. My friend was right: more than fifty emails arrived within the first twelve hours, and I began a process that felt akin to online shoe shopping. (Too shiny, too tight…)

It was a wild experiment for a number of reasons. At that time, it was impossible to separate the triangulation of feelings I was experiencing regarding my: a) anger and jealousy about my lack of penis, b) desire to have a penis that *I* can feel and c) desire to have sex with someone who has a penis *they* can feel.

How's that for a flow chart? Sometimes I just want sex to be easier.

I arranged to meet a handsome man a few days later. Five minutes into our *still fully clothed* hangout, he finished

132 | SECOND LIFE

unexpectedly on account of being overexcited, apologized and left the room to clean up. I tried to crack jokes to make him feel better and offered to get him a drink.

Fantasy, indeed.

Mike

Intercourse belongs to the body I used to have, in my once and former life, before I became positive. I would like to return to every lost pleasure, or at least offer summery descriptions, but too many years have gone by. What I remember instead are the years of fearful touches after I became positive, when my partners and I turned to face an early death. *Why have you brought me this terrible disease? At the very moment when I open myself to you, I could become infected and die.* Having sex used to mean the movie theatre or the park, alleyways and front lawns, but now the more controlled environment of the bedroom was preferred. Some new sense of privacy entered our lives, along with new feelings of shame. In the many years before the cocktail arrived to offer some of us the chance of a second life, what was required above all was safety and control. And while that reliably ensured that my partners would remain uninfected, it wasn't a recipe for sexy.

Carie showed me that my hands could reach all the way across her bruised sexual life, all the way back to the rapist who had plotted revenge on her older sister by courting Carie slowly and systematically, and then violently raping her as soon as she turned eighteen. Happy birthday! We replayed each gesture without having to learn the score – somehow her body was able to offer up every cue, whispering how hard and how much and how often. Only this time the unwanted cocktail of arousal and violation was newly mixed with a healing tenderness. For the unwanted gift of showing her what she wanted, she pursued me with a terrifying rigour, determined to remind us both that some nights last the rest of your life. Once again I learned that if sex was not reasonable and contained, safe in every sense of the word, the result could only be plague years.

Today the fantasy is not intercourse, which feels too much like a commitment, or the culmination of someone else's dream, but sperm. For most of my life it has been the dreaded carrier of contagion. Little wonder then that my fantasies should convert the fearful into the erotic – at night I slip into the milky way and drink deeply. How did Melville, the great American sperm chronicler put it? 'There's hogsheads of sperm ahead, Mr. Stubb, and that's what ye came for. (Pull, my boys!) Sperm, sperm's the play! This at least is duty; duty and profit hand in hand!'

Chase

She was the most beautiful girl I had ever seen, with eyes capable of holding the kind of contact that inspired instant, fearless fantasy. It was rumoured that she was in a relationship with a woman at school, and such a rare, same-sex affirming sound bite provided the only encouragement I needed to start orienting my feelings. Unrequited affection affords unlimited opportunities for future – albeit sometimes fictitious – projection and planning. If she could be with that woman, then she could be with me.

One day, I left a message on her answering machine playfully listing facts I deemed relevant to our connection, the most important and obvious of which being that I was different from her other suitors on account of being a woman. She responded a few hours later saying that she was – contrary to popular belief – only interested in men, and therefore not interested in me. The adrenaline of embarrassment and rejection surged through my veins silently. She was a glass of Coke, and I was a dirty penny.

As years passed, our relationship settled into the well-fixed contours of meaningful and long-standing friendship, and I honed an ability to distinguish between love's effects and love's realities. It is indeed possible for someone to be the subject of your own secret version of *The Notebook* while also remaining fulfilled in other contexts – a skill I now believe is the result of learning to love someone more, rather than resigning to love them less.

Long after transitioning, while camping on the outskirts of a once familiar town, our casual and familiar bed sharing suddenly shifted context. For forty-eight hours our relationship was transported, rendering the fantasy no longer a fiction and revealing connections that were long considered but never actually spoken. When the trip was over, things between us settled down again – it was a strangely satisfying, yet knowingly unrepeatable flash in love's most prestigious pan. I tried to talk to her about what had happened in the days that followed, but there was nothing left to be said. Second lives might afford second chances, but some of our stories will find similar ends.

Mike

I wonder if I could introduce my newest fave writer into the conversation. Her name is Hannah Black, and she writes sentences that glow in the dark. Here is the finale of her *New Inquiry* essay called 'You Are Too Much.'

> Correct attachments are for the White Family; for the rest of us – people of color, queers, queers of color, single women. and so on, that whole mixed and conflicted bag of lives – there 's whatever we can make do with, there are brief moments and long memories, there is daydream and pop music. For the White Family love is health, but for us love is at once a symbol of a possible future, a vanishing present, and the sign of the patriarchal white permafrost that threatens to destroy us. If we are ambivalent about love in its present form, it is only because, against the odds, we choose to feel something other than hatred.
>
> Girl, you have always done too much or too little, and you are always too much or too little already. You are a mess of emotions. you live hand-to-mouth and from one day to the next, the slightest touch sends you into raptures or turns you cold as ice. It's an achieved miracle, a form of heroism, that you still consent to be touched at all.

Chase

The smarter I get, the less I understand love's particularities. Even a rudimentary understanding of political power structures can make love feel like a socially constructed trap. Of course, I say that to you with as much clarity and certainty as I can manage, while admitting that my favourite movie genre is romantic comedy. Love is the battleground where all past wounds and survivals play out. One cannot be on a teeter-totter alone, and heartbreak provides such a reliable counter-weight to new excitement.

After my final breakup conversation with Sam – forever remembered as heartbreak number one – I cried so hard leaving his house that I had to pull the car over. I think about that moment often, in part because the radio songs attached to that crying were so embarrassing, and in part because I remember feeling something inside me break. I remember thinking, 'This is what love feels like.'

I've recently met someone new. We live in different cities, so our process of getting to know each other has largely been via email and text. In some ways, the distance is welcome because we can't forgo logic in favour of endorphin-based decision-making; it also lets us disclose things about ourselves that we might otherwise try to repackage or forget. Having both just ended long-term relationships, neither one of us is feeling particularly clear as to our next steps. That said, I'm pretty sure one of my next steps should be making out with her, though we haven't got there in conversation yet.

I decided to send her a book. She recently described feeling submerged in post-breakup processing, and I thought some well-curated fiction might be a welcome gift. My sister, the most well-versed fiction reader I know, has become my number-one resource. I write, 'Okay, so I'm trying to pick a book for someone who has just gone through a breakup, but whom I'd also like to date. What book says "Breakups are miserable!" and "Love is totally worth it!" simultaneously?'

My sister's response, 'I am currently reading *The Days of Abandonment*.' Touché. When you type 'books about love' into a search engine, the auto-fill predictions give you: 'and loss,' 'and life,' 'and cancer.' 'Maybe you should send her *Bad Feminist* by Roxane Gay,' she adds. Not a bad idea.

I understand that this book will function as a stand-in for various thoughts and gestures currently left unsaid. Because what I want to communicate to her is the kind of lover I am, but I will do so through the guise of being an attentive-from-a-distance friend. Instead of being forthright with my intentions, I will plant seeds in an otherwise flora-less garden, and wait for water and sunlight to attend – anything to not have to pull the car over when eventually driving away.

Just today, she sent me a message to say that the relationship she had recently ended was in fact not yet ready to end. And while she acknowledged and validated the fire between us, her note arrived just in time to recalibrate our new context as friends.

Every John Cusack movie reminds me that love is possible, and every Kevin Spacey film takes that feeling away. 'There's a package waiting for you at 192 Books on 10th Ave. No rush or response needed,' my note to her would have said.

Mike

The confessional returns as seduction machine, or even the relationship that I won't let myself have. Because you're living in another city, Chase, you're far enough away so that I can get close to you. It has struck me more than once that I'm able to write things to you that I can't manage to say out loud even to my closest comrades. As if the most private thoughts needed to be reserved for the public, and you were the gateway drug to that public. Did I say drug? I meant of course mother and father, brother and sister, the whole tangled family of love. The more you write me, the more I need to hear.

2.13
Curtain Call

Chase

Living a second life offered me an opportunity to do things better. I had second guesses, second sight and many second chances. But this is a partially imagined fiction, as one of the greatest costs of second living is an inability to believe your own tales. Does it make me more or less romantic that I now use phrases such as 'I will never love like that again'? After all, I do know that I continue to love, and that nothing ever really happens 'again.' Even my desire to proclaim comfort in the unresolved or the unstable feels like the construction of a new fiction. Do you ever feel that way?

Mike

When the HIV drugs arrived and the certainty of an early death was snatched away, I lost the container that I had grown accustomed to furnishing with all of my favourite things. My reindeers of sadness and shame, disgust and anxiety. That container was a story that allowed me to endure the plague years, and allows me to ride out this time as well. When does a life sentence sound like a death sentence? Now that I'm on the other side of the rainbow, with brave new generations of pharmaceuticals to keep the shape-shifting virus at bay, I have been granted a second life. So why am I still paused here before the door of this cherished promise, so many years later, as if I were performing a real-time rendition of Kafka's 'Before the Law'? In this brief parable, a man offers the doorkeeper to the law all he has in order to enter, and is met by this inscrutable reply: 'I am only taking it to keep you from thinking you have omitted anything.' For years the man waits by the door – promising, bargaining, begging – but the situation never changes. He wonders why others haven't chanced by and tried the entranceway, but it turns out the door exists for him alone.

After Mark died, I ended the relationship I was in, too tired to hold up my end of the arguments any longer, and then plunged into a five-year haze of depression. There were endless work horizons and a prohibition against being touched. And then Don killed himself, my first best friend, born on the same sunny afternoon in the same city as me. Babz was gone a few months later, and then Tom. They feel more real than breakfast, more urgent than the surviving friends I embrace in between bouts of computer dedications. Whenever I feel them throwing their voices into mine, I long again for a container. The voguers call it 'striking a pose.' The Buddhists name it 'setting an intention.' The promise that rolls me out of the dreamwork each morning is that I will smile through fourteen more summers before leaving the building and joining my dead friends. While so many fairytales have come and gone, this one continues to provide necessary consolations.

Chase

A few years ago, a well-known trans activist in Toronto killed himself, sending shockwaves again through our community. I find myself unable to stop thinking about our collective suicidal tendencies. People keep dying. Suicide is rampant. Every trans person I know carries stories and histories with suicide, either within themselves or with friends. We are consistently reminded that the simple promise of *more* – more breakfasts, more misunderstandings, more weekends – might not be good enough reason to live.

Even as I continue to read through the online blogs and diaries, I believe that staying alive is one of the most powerful and provocative forms of public representation. Particularly when there are so many others who would rather see people like us dead. Kate Bornstein's thesis reverberates again and again: stay alive. How do we make it possible for us to stay alive? We continue waking up in a world that sees our living as inherently confrontational. The mere choice to live in public – even the new public of the Internet – is considered an invitation to attack. To this day, when I walk out of the bathroom at a movie theatre, my mom asks, 'Is everything okay?'

If we can create containers that hold on to our best selves, while also making room for the shadows and shame, perhaps we might survive the death sentence of our first lives and change the rules of second-life living. Do you remember the first time we met? Before that moment, I had only known you through your movies, the skilfully crafted portraits you design intentionally for the world to see. But your body is a space that transforms the life of your projects and revolutionizes the potential for others to see and feel seen. I realize now that this kind of writing calls for a new kind of attention, an off-the-page, behind-the-scenes engagement wherein I convince you to keep living.

What I hear in your writing is a longing, not for death, but for the release from disappointment. Perhaps that is what our second life keeps proving over and over again: that we can endure disappointment by changing our descriptions.

They have grown tired of airplanes, even the promise of being somewhere else delivers only the feeling of duty. They decide to meet in the faraway place they call home. Chase picks the destination, a caffeinated hideaway in the city's forbidden east end. It's wintertime, so Mike wears what looks like a sleeping bag stuffed with pillows while Chase is also nearly unrecognizable. They order double shots of espresso and make their way to the windows, where the good light finds them. The sound of boots rubbing against rubber, the city exhaling its chill every time the door opens. The barista dances with her eyes closed to her favourite song. The sound of a newspaper left behind. They might wait a long time before saying anything at all.

And then Chase begins: 'I want you to promise me something.'

'You're not going to ask me to have fun, are you? You know I don't like having fun.'

'Nothing so drastic. I just need you to stay on your meds. I know the new batch has been giving you so many problems, I know you haven't slept for the last month, but it's the only way ...'

And suddenly from the corners of Chase's brown eyes appear hints of water. His brows crease in a furrowed puzzle wearing silent questions: what is happening to me? Who am I? Mike wants to throw his arms around his newly dissolving friend but is afraid to break eye contact; he can feel his hands starting to shake again because that's where the unspoken words live.

The other names of Chris Marker – ones he self-assigned to render himself fiction – come to Mike in a tumble: Sergei

Murasaki, Kosinski, Sandor Krasna. He chooses Kosinski and stands up.

Chase stands up too, drawn from the same chord.

They hold each other without having to say the words.

Not the end.

Acknowledgements

Chase

I have friends who have remained with me in this life through all versions. I am forever and loyally indebted to Rebekah Skoor and Bryce Longton for companionship that has transcended significant time, growth and meaningful space. To Mona Tavakoli, Becky Gebhardt, Amber Elliot and Chaska Potter for continuing to be the brightest lights in Los Angeles. I am grateful to Riva Lehrer, Amanda Flynn and M. K. Bryson for allowing our interrelated lives and shared spaces to appear so visibly in this book. To Kate Bornstein for modelling years of strategic public vulnerability as a form of impassioned politicized resistance and survival. To Lauren Berlant, Jasbir Puar, Michelle Stone, Jen Richards and Tey Meadow, who each inhabit spaces of curiosity and possibility that rarely rely on geography to be maintained. Zoe Whittall and Vivek Shraya make the interconnected projects of writing and friendship feel expansive, collective and possible. Kaleb Robertson, Jen Markowitz, Hannah Dyer, Casey Mecija, Gabby Moser, Allyson Mitchell and Deirdre Logue continue to charge Toronto with incomparable grounding and inspirational fire. To Naomi de Szegheo-Lang for necessary reminders about worlds beyond this one and the inimitable beauty of a third-round story edit.

Writing nonfiction – whatever that means – is a precarious and emotional endeavour. I am grateful to my parents for not only allowing but also wholeheartedly supporting snapshots of a life lived by so many to be revealed in this way. This book is for Kristen Schilt and Sarah Lyndsay who make innumerable versions of life, love and family feel possible.

Mike

Thanks to Catherine Bush, whose narrative wisdoms helped give this book a shape, to Judy Rebick for her easygoing courage examples, and Pat Rockman for grinning at monsters.

Chase

We are grateful to Michelle Tea, Maggie Nelson, John Greyson and Chris Kraus for taking chances on this new and ever-evolving work; your early words of encouragement lit fires. Working with Alana Wilcox is like winning the literary lottery, how could we be so lucky? Thanks to the team at Coach House Books for helping our project take flight. We remain in full support of mixed metaphors.

Portions of this book have appeared in *Original Plumbing* online, *POV* and *Psychoanalysis, Culture and Society*.

The authors are grateful to Hannah Black for permission to reproduce an excerpt from 'You Are Too Much,' published online in *The New Inquiry*.

01 Still

Baldwin, James. *The Devil Finds Work: An Essay*. New York: The Dial Press, 1976.

Barthes, Roland. *Camera Lucida: Reflections on Photography*. 1st American edition. New York: Hill and Wang, 1981.

Berlant, Lauren, and David Seitz. 'Interview with Lauren Berlant.' Society and Space, 2013: online.

Black, Hannah. 'You Are Too Much.' *The New Inquiry* (April 1, 2014): online.

Butler, Judith. *Undoing Gender*. New York: Routledge, 2004.

Carson, Anne. 'Variations on the Right to Remain Silent.' *A Public Space* 7 (2008): online.

Ferrante, Elena. *The Days of Abandonment*. New York: Europa Editions, 2005.

Gay, Roxane. *Bad Feminist*. New York: Harper Collins, 2014.

Gladwell, Malcolm. *Outliers: The Story of Success*. New York: Little, Brown and Co., 2008.

Gozlan, Oren. 'The Accident of Gender.' Special Section - Online-Only Book Review Supplement. *The Psychoanalytic Review* 95, no. 4 (2008): 541–570.

Green, Jamison. *Becoming a Visible Man*. Nashville, TN: Vanderbilt University Press, 2004.

Kafka, Franz. *The Trial*. Translated by David Wyllie. Mineola, NY: Dover Publications, 2009.

Koestenbaum, Wayne. 'Speaking in the Shadow of AIDS.' In *The State of the Language*, edited by Christopher Ricks and Leonard Michaels, 163–170. Berkeley, CA: University of California Press, 1990.

Melville, Herman. *Moby-Dick; or The Whale*. New York: Harper & Brothers, 1851.

Nelson, Maggie. *The Argonauts*. Minneapolis, MN: Graywolf Press, 2015.

Phillips, Adam. *Becoming Freud: The Making of a Psychoanalyst*. New Haven, CT: Yale University Press, 2014.

Preciado, Paul B. *Testo Junkie: Sex, Drugs, and Biopolitics in the Pharmacopornographic Era*. Translated by Bruce Benderson. New York: Feminist Press, 2013

Rankine, Claudia. *Citizen: An American Lyric*. Minneapolis, MN: Graywolf Press, 2014.

Turner, Ricky. 'Pharmacopornography: An nterview with Beatriz Preciado.' *The Paris Review*. December 4, 2013: online.

02 Moving

Akin (2012) by Chase Joynt
Deconstructing Harry (1997) by Woody Allen
The Flying Nun (TV Series, 1967–1970), Multiple Directors
La Jetée (1962) by Chris Marker
Mark (2010) by Mike Hoolboom
Positiv (1998) by Mike Hoolboom
Remembrance of Things to Come (2003) by Chris Marker
Resisterectomy (2012) by Chase Joynt and Dr. M. K. Bryson
Sans Soleil (1983) by Chris Marker

Chase Joynt

Chase Joynt is a Toronto-based moving-image artist and writer. Recently awarded the EP Canada/Canada Film Capital Award for Emerging Canadian Artist and jury awards for Best Documentary and Best Short, Chase's work continues to be exhibited internationally. As a recipient of a Mellon Fellowship in Arts Practice and Scholarship at the University of Chicago, Chase's recent speaking engagements include Harvard University, Princeton University, The New York Academy of Medicine, and the Museum of Contemporary Art, Chicago. Chase holds a BA from the UCLA School of Theater Film and Television, and is a PhD candidate in Film at York University where he holds a Provost Disseratation Scholarship.   www.chasejoynt.com

Mike Hoolboom

Born: Korean War, the pill, hydrogen bomb, playboy mansion. 1980s: Film emulsion fetish and diary salvos. Schooling at the Funnel: collective avant-geek cine utopia. 1990s: experimentalist features, transgressive psychodramas, questions of nationalism. 2000s: Seroconversion cyborg (life after death), film-to-video transcode: feature-length-found-footage bios. Fringe media archaeologist: copyleft author 7 books, co/editor 12 books. Curator: 30 programs + www.fringeonline.ca Occasional employments: artistic director Images Fest, fringe distribution Canadian Filmmakers. 75 film/vids, most redacted. 10 features. 30 awards, 14 international retrospectives. 2 lifetime achievement awards.

www.mikehoolboom.com

About the
Exploded Views Series

Exploded Views is a series of probing, provocative essays that offer surprising perspectives on the most intriguing cultural issues and figures of our day. Longer than a typical magazine article but shorter than a full-length book, these are punchy salvos written by some of North America's most lyrical journalists and critics. Spanning a variety of forms and genres – history, biography, polemic, commentary – and published simultaneously in all digital formats and handsome, collectible print editions, this is literary reportage that at once investigates, illuminates and intervenes.

www.chbooks.com/explodedviews

Typeset in Goodchild Pro and Gibson Pro. Goodchild was designed by Nick Shinn in 2002 at his ShinnType foundry in Orangeville, Ontario. Shinn's design takes its inspiration from French printer Nicholas Jenson who, at the height of the Renaissance in Venice, used the basic Carolingian minuscule calligraphic hand and classic roman inscriptional capitals to arrive at a typeface that produced a clear and even texture that most literate Europeans could read. Shinn's design captures the calligraphic feel of Jensen's early types in a more refined digital format. Gibson was designed by Rod McDonald in honour of John Gibson FGDC (1928–2011), Rod's long-time friend and one of the founders of the Society of Graphic Designers of Canada. It was McDonald's intention to design a solid, contemporary and affordable sans serif face.

Printed at the old Coach House on bpNichol Lane in Toronto, Ontario, on Rolland Opaque Natural paper, which was manufactured, acid-free, in Saint-Jérôme, Quebec, from 50 percent recycled paper, and it was printed with vegetable-based ink on a 1965 Heidelberg KORD offset litho press. Its pages were folded on a Baumfolder, gathered by hand, bound on a Sulby Auto-Minabinda and trimmed on a Polar single-knife cutter.

Edited by Alana Wilcox
Cover by Ingrid Paulson
Chase's author photo by David Hawe

Coach House Books
80 bpNichol Lane
Toronto ON M5S 3J4
Canada

416 979 2217
800 367 6360

mail@chbooks.com
www.chbooks.com